FOUNDATIONAL

ORDER AND HUMAN ORIGINS

Creation Order, the First Humanity, and the Emergence of the Second Humanity

MBRS Book3 — Master-Level Formation

The Official Student Textbook

DR. YERAL E. OGANDO

FOUNDATIONAL ORDER AND HUMAN ORIGINS

The Official Student Textbook for the Master of Biblical Restoration Studies (MBRS)

By

Dr. Yeral E. Ogando

Authored and published by

Dr. Yeral E. Ogando

Adopted for instructional use by

Yahuah Institute of Biblical Restoration, Inc.

As the core text for

The Master of Biblical Restoration Studies (MBRS) Program

Scripture quotations are taken exclusively from Dabar Yahuah Scriptures – www.yahuahbible.com.

This textbook is produced for academic, instructional, and theological training purposes within the MBRS program and affiliated courses.

"All instructional texts used by the MBRS Program are independently authored and published by Dr. Yeral E. Ogando. The Institute adopts these texts solely for instructional purposes and does not own, publish, or receive revenue from them."

ISBN: 978-1-946249-51-7

1. AUTHORIZATION & INSTITUTIONAL STATEMENT

This textbook, Foundations of Biblical Restoration, is authored and published by Dr. Yeral E. Ogando and is adopted and approved for instructional use by Yahuah Institute of Biblical Restoration, Inc. as the core instructional text for the Master of Biblical Restoration Studies (MBRS) program.

All doctrinal positions, terminology, instructional structures, and evaluative standards contained within this volume are governed exclusively by Dabar Yahuah Scriptures as preserved in the Scriptures recognized by the Institute: the inspired writings of the Tanakh (Old Testament), the preserved Apokryfos, and the Renewed Covenant (New Testament) writings.

This text operates within a closed canonical and theological framework for the academic cycle in which it is issued. No external denominational systems, philosophical methodologies, speculative Yada Yahuah (theology), or institutional traditions are permitted to govern interpretation, instruction, or assessment within the MBRS program.

This Student Edition is authorized for instructional use solely within the MBRS program.

Unauthorized reproduction, distribution, or use outside of Institute-approved instructional contexts is prohibited.

2. PREFACE & STATEMENT OF PURPOSE

Foundations of Biblical Restoration exists because Scripture itself demands restoration.

This textbook was not written to defend denominational systems, preserve inherited theology, or harmonize philosophical frameworks with Scripture. It was written to allow **Dabar Yahuah** to govern Yada Yahuah (theology) without competition.

Modern theology often begins with assumptions and searches Scripture for support. Restoration Yada Yahuah (theology) reverses that order. Scripture establishes authority, defines categories, diagnoses corruption, and reveals restoration according to divine intent rather than human tradition.

This book serves as the **single, integrated instructional text** for the Master of Biblical Restoration Studies (MBRS). It guides the student from Scriptural Witness through, *Yahuah: Restoration Guide*, the *Origin of Evil: Biblical Truths Hidden in Plain Sight*, the **Three Humanities™**: *The Division of Humanity in Yahuah's Plan* - Volume 1, and th*e Three Humanities™*: *The Restoration of the First Humanity in Yahuah's Plan*—culminating in independent thesis defense.

3. STATEMENT OF PURPOSE

The purpose of this textbook is to:

>Establish Scripture as the sole governing authority
>Restore biblical categories obscured by tradition and translation
>Define evil without attributing corruption to Yahuah
>Explain humanity through the **Three Humanities™** framework
>Present restoration as transformation, not repair
>Prepare students to defend **Restoration Yada Yahuah** (theology)

independently and accurately

This text is not devotional. It is not speculative. It is instructional, corrective, and authoritative.

4. PROGRAM LEARNING OUTCOMES
MASTER OF BIBLICAL RESTORATION STUDIES (MBRS)

Upon successful completion of the MBRS program, the student will be able to:

1.Demonstrate Covenantal Reasoning across the full body of Scripture, integrating the Tanakh (Old Testament), Apokryfos, and Renewed Covenant (New Testament) writings without contradiction.

2.**Explain Scriptural authorit**y as divinely originated, canonically bounded, and covenantal preserved.

3.Define evil, corruption, judgment, and restoration using Scriptural categories alone, without reliance on philosophical or denominational frameworks.

4.**Articulate the Three Humanities™ framework** (First, Second, Third Humanities and the Variant) using Scripture-governed anthropology and lineage Yada Yahuah (theology).

5.**Distinguish between sin, corruption, and Creational alteration**, explaining why restoration requires transformation rather than moral repair.

6.**Apply covenant language discipline responsibly,** demonstrating how words govern doctrine and prevent theological distortion.

7.**Defend Restoration Yada Yahuah (theology)** from creation to consummation as a unified, Scripture-consistent system.

8.**Produce and defend a master-level thesis** grounded exclusively in Scripture, demonstrating doctrinal clarity, canonical consistency, and methodological integrity.

5. HOW TO USE THIS TEXTBOOK

This textbook is designed for **structured, sequential use** within the MBRS program.

STUDENT RESPONSIBILITIES

- Read all assigned Scripture before engaging commentary or explanations.
- Follow the progression of weeks and months without skipping sections.
- Use only Institute-approved Scriptural sources when completing assignments.
- Adhere strictly to locked templates, prompts, and evaluation criteria.

- Demonstrate mastery through clarity, Scripture use, and disciplined reasoning.

INSTRUCTIONAL STRUCTURE

- Each Term builds upon previous authority and doctrine.
- Each Month introduces defined instructional goals.
- Each Week focuses on specific Scriptural concepts.
- Assessments measure integration and reasoning, not memorization.

This text is not designed for casual reading.
It is designed for **formation, correction, and qualification.**

Students who attempt to bypass structure, introduce external systems, or rely on speculation will not advance.

6. ACADEMIC & SCRIPTURAL INTEGRITY STATEMENT

Enrollment in the MBRS program constitutes agreement to the following standards:
- **Scripture governs all conclusions.**
- **Dabar Yahuah is the highest authority.**
- No denominational, philosophical, or speculative systems may override Scripture.
- All work must be original, truthful, and accurately cited.
- Plagiarism, doctrinal innovation, or misrepresentation of Scripture results in disqualification.
- Advancement is evaluative, not automatic.

This program values **clarity over creativity**, **submission over speculation, and truth over tradition.**

The goal is not affirmation, but formation.

Authorized Textual Resources and Access

The instructional texts and Scriptural resources referenced within the Master of Biblical Restoration Studies (MBRS) program are made available through designated platforms.

Primary reference texts and supporting source materials authored by Dr. Yeral E. Ogando are openly accessible at www.yahuahdabar.com. These materials may be read online by any visitor. Registration allows users to download PDF versions of the source texts. These materials are publicly available and are not restricted to enrolled students.

The Dabar Yahuah Scriptures, including the Tanakh (Old Testament), Apokryfos, and Renewed Covenant (New Testament) writings, are openly accessible for online reading at www.yahuahbible.com. These texts are provided as the authorized Scriptural reference for the MBRS program and are available to all readers.

For Scriptural study and term-level consultation, students are instructed to use the Dabar Yahuah Scriptures App, including its Strong Concordance tools for Hebrew and Greek reference. This tool is used for confirming word forms, meanings, and Scriptural usage in alignment with the Institute's instructional framework.

The Student Edition textbooks, however, are not publicly distributed through these websites. Student textbooks are provided through the Institute's instructional platform or authorized course distribution channels, with the exception of the Amazon print edition.

These access distinctions are intentional and form part of the Institute's instructional and evaluative framework.

Contents

TERM III — *THE THREE HUMANITIES*™
MASTER-LEVEL PROPER · PINNACLE STUDIES
Graduate Formation · Terms III–IV

Academic Orientation — Term III · Month 1

Term III marks the formal entrance into the Master-level proper phase of study within the Yahuah Institute of Biblical Restoration, Inc. This phase presupposes the successful completion of Term I (Associate-Level Foundations) and Term II (Bachelor-Level Formation), including demonstrated mastery of:

- Scriptural authority and canon hierarchy
- Covenantal reasoning and continuity
- Jurisdictional reading of creation and history
- Methodological discipline within Yada' Yahuah

At this level, foundational debates are no longer revisited. Terms III and IV together constitute the pinnacle of the program, devoted to advanced analysis of creation order, humanity, corruption, judgment, and restoration as revealed through Scripture. These terms assume precision, restraint, and fidelity to sequence.

The Three Humanities™ — Term III Scope

Term III initiates The Three Humanities™, the central construct of the Master curriculum.

Month 1 is devoted entirely to Book One, The Three Humanities™: The 22 Works of Creation, which establishes the divine foundation of all reality.
This month addresses creation at its highest level of order and intention. It teaches that creation does not begin with Adam, nor even with the material earth, but with divine intention, spoken authority, and pre-material spiritual realities. The purpose of Month 1 is not description, but orientation: it trains

the student how to read creation correctly before any discussion of deviation is permitted.

Methodological Boundary — Month 1
During Month 1:
- No discussion of sin, rebellion, corruption, Edenic failure, judgment, or redemption is permitted
- No retrojection of later categories into the creation week is allowed
- Creation must be read as perfect, intentional, ordered, bounded, filled, governed, and complete

These themes belong to later months and cannot be understood correctly unless creation is first established as lacking nothing. Any attempt to interpret corruption before establishing completion constitutes methodological error.

Academic Expectations at the Master Level
Students are required to reason with maximum precision. Assumptions inherited from:
- Religious tradition
- Philosophical anthropology
- Scientific reductionism

must be suspended. Scripture alone defines created order, agency, sequence, and purpose. At this stage, students are not permitted to harmonize Scripture with external systems; they must allow Scripture to govern interpretation internally.

Required Outcomes — End of Month 1
By the conclusion of Month 1, the student must clearly demonstrate understanding that:
- Creation unfolds through ordered divine works, not chaos
- Spiritual realities precede physical manifestation
- Humanity's origin is rooted in divine intention, not biological emergence
- Man and woman are created within a perfected and bounded system

- Shabbâth crowns creation as sanctified completion, not recovery from labor
- The work of Yahuah Êlôhîym is perfect and lacking nothing

These are not thematic conclusions; they are interpretive controls.

Programmatic Consequence

Month 1 establishes the non-negotiable baseline for all subsequent study of humanity, corruption, judgment, and restoration within the Master-level Yadaʿ Yahuah curriculum.

Failure to internalize and preserve the interpretive boundaries of Month 1 compromises all later material in The Three Humanities™ and requires formal remediation before advancement to Month 2.

UNDERSTANDING THE DIVINE FOUNDATION OF ALL THINGS
Order Before Matter

PURPOSE OF WEEK 33
Week 33 functions as orientation, not information.

Chapters 1 and 2 of The Three Humanities™ establish the interpretive ground rules for everything that follows. Before humanity, rebellion, corruption, judgment, or restoration can be read correctly, the student must learn how Scripture defines origin, priority, and authority.

This week corrects a persistent Yada Yahuah error:
the assumption that material manifestation marks the beginning of reality. Scripture, read sequentially and covenantally, identifies a different starting point:
ordered speech, spiritual administration, and assigned existence precede all physical form.

The goal of Week 33 is not persuasion, but interpretive discipline. Students must learn to read creation without collapsing spirit into body, appearance into origin, or manifestation into identity.

GOVERNING SCRIPTURAL ANCHORS
(Chapters 1–2 — The Three Humanities)
The following texts function as juridical anchors, fixing sequence and priority. They are not prooftexts; they establish interpretive boundaries.
- Berēshīṯ (Genesis) 1:1–5 — speech establishes order before filling
- Tehillim (Psalm) 33:6–9 — creation responds to command, not force
- Yôḥanan (John) 1:1–4 — meaning and life precede material existence
- ʿÊber (Hebrews) 11:3 — the visible proceeds from the unseen
- Iyôb (Job) 38:4–7 — heavenly beings present before earth's completion

- Zakaryahu (Zechariah) 12:1 — spirits are formed by Yahuah, not generated by flesh
- Qoheleth (Ecclesiastes) 12:7 — spirit returns to its giver, not to matter

Together, these texts establish priority, pre-existence, and jurisdiction without contradiction.

Teaching Explanation

Chapters 1 and 2 train the student to read Scripture according to foundational order.

The governing lesson is not what was created, but when and why priority is assigned.

Scripture presents the following interpretive hierarchy:
- Speech precedes structure
- Spiritual administration precedes environment
- Existence precedes embodiment
- Assignment precedes manifestation

Day One is therefore not an introduction, but a control point. By assigning the creation of all angels and all human spirits (from beginning to end) to the first day, Scripture prevents later confusion between identity and biology.

The 22 Works of Creation, distributed across six days, function as an anti-collapse mechanism. They forbid the reader from treating creation, formation, and activation as a single event.

Interpretive error begins when this structure is ignored.

Order as the First Principle of Yada Yahuah

Yada Yahuah does not begin with matter, observation, or outcome.

It begins with order and assignment.

By establishing spiritual reality first, Scripture fixes:
- who may act
- where action is permitted

- when manifestation is lawful

This explains why later corruption is not accidental but jurisdictional.
Boundaries matter because order existed before bodies did.
Any reading that treats physical form as origin will misread rebellion, judgment, and restoration.

Alignment Focus — Chapters 1–2 (The Three Humanities)

By the end of Week 33, students must retain the following interpretive conclusions:

- Day One governs interpretation, not chronology alone
- All spirits are created before bodies appear
- The 22 Works preserve lawful distinction between stages of creation
- Structure precedes habitation as a rule, not an exception
- Boundaries define authority, not limitation

These are not doctrines to memorize; they are reading controls to apply throughout the book.

KEY TERMS — WEEK 33

- Yada Yahuah
  Restored knowledge derived from Scriptural order, covenantal structure, and lawful sequence.
- Foundational Order
  That which is established first and therefore governs all later interpretation.
- Pre-Manifest Existence
  Existence assigned by Yahuah prior to physical appearance in time.

COVENANTAL STUDY TASK
Using Scripture and Chapters 1–2 only:
•Identify how Scriptural sequence establishes priority without explanation
•Demonstrate why Day One must interpret later embodiment
•Explain how the 22 Works prevent category confusion
•Distinguish clearly between being created, being formed, and being manifested

Avoid abstraction. Your analysis must remain text-governed and sequential.

FINAL THOUGHTS — WEEK 33

Creation does not begin where humans first observe it.

It begins where Yahuah first assigns it.

If students learn to read from order to manifestation, they will not confuse bodies with identity, nor history with origin.

QUOTE REFLECTION

"What is assigned first governs what appears later."

THE GREAT WORK OF THE FIRMAMENT
Separation, Authority, and Structure

PURPOSE OF WEEK 34
Week 34 functions as structural clarification, not narrative expansion. Chapters 3 and 4 advance the interpretive discipline established in Week 33 by demonstrating how separation operates as the architecture of life. Creation does not progress by accumulation, but by assignment through division.

This week corrects a recurring Yada Yahuah error:
the assumption that separation is a response to corruption.
Scripture establishes separation before sin, before humanity, and before conflict. Separation is not punitive; it is foundational. Without it, life cannot function, time cannot be measured, and authority cannot be exercised.

The goal of Week 34 is coherence:
students must learn to recognize separation as intentional structure, not fragmentation.

Governing Scriptural Anchors
(Chapters 3–4 — The Three Humanities)
The following texts function as juridical anchors, fixing separation as a condition of order:
- Berēshīth (Genesis) 1:6–8 — division of waters establishes realms
- Berēshīth (Genesis) 1:9–13 — land appears only after waters are restrained
- Berēshīth (Genesis) 1:14–19 — light is governed, not merely created
- Tehillim (Psalm) 19:1–4 — the heavens communicate order, not chaos
- Iyôb (Job) 26:7–10 — boundaries are marked by authority
- Yasha'yahu (Isaiah) 40:21–22 — creation is measured and governed

Together, these texts establish that separation precedes life, function, and timekeeping.

Teaching Explanation

Chapters 3 and 4 train the student to read creation as architectural progression.

The governing principle is consistent:
- Nothing flourishes until it is separated
- Nothing is governed until it is assigned
- Nothing functions until boundaries are enforced

Day 3 demonstrates that land cannot become productive until waters are gathered and restrained.

Day 4 demonstrates that time cannot function until light is regulated and measured.

Separation, therefore, is not absence—it is structure.

This explains why later rebellion is always described as boundary violation, not innovation. Mixture is never creative in Scripture; it is destructive because it dismantles structure that existed before life emerged.

Separation as Authority, Not Conflict

Within Yada Yahuah, separation establishes:
- jurisdiction (what belongs where)
- function (what operates when)
- accountability (what may not cross)

Heaven is not earth.

Light is not darkness.

Day is not night.

These distinctions are not negotiable, because they are commanded, not discovered.

Chapters 3 and 4 demonstrate that life appears only after separation is complete, and prosperity continues only while separation is maintained.

Alignment Focus — Chapters 3–4 (The Three Humanities)

By the end of Week 34, students must retain the following interpretive conclusions:

- Separation precedes life, not sin
- Boundaries are commanded, not emergent
- The firmament is structure, not emptiness
- Time exists because light is regulated, not blended
- Mixing realms produces corruption, not progress

These are not abstract principles; they are reading controls for understanding rebellion, judgment, and restoration later in the text.

KEY TERMS — WEEK 34

- Firmament
  The structured expanse that assigns realms by divine command.
- Separation
  Division established by Yahuah to preserve order, function, and life.
- Boundary
  A limit that enables purpose and jurisdiction rather than restriction.

COVENANTAL STUDY TASK

Using Scripture and Chapters 3–4 only:
•Identify how separation functions as assignment rather than division
•Demonstrate why life requires restraint before expansion
•Explain how time depends on regulated light
•Trace how later corruption assumes the violation of pre-existing boundaries
Do not generalize. Remain sequential and text-governed.

FINAL THOUGHTS — WEEK 34

Creation does not advance by mixture.

It advances by separation rightly maintained.

When boundaries are honored, life flourishes.

When boundaries are crossed, corruption follows.

QUOTE REFLECTION

"Where separation is enforced, order can endure."

TERM III · MONTH 1 — WEEK 35
THE CREATION OF EARTHLY REALMS AND HUMANITY
Life Within Order

PURPOSE OF WEEK 35

Week 35 functions as placement clarification, not narrative continuation. Chapters 5 and 6 demonstrate that life is introduced only after order is complete, and that Scripture treats living beings not as emergent phenomena, but as assigned populations within defined realms.

This week corrects a persistent Yada Yahuah error:

the assumption that life generates order.

Scripture presents the opposite sequence: order precedes life, and life flourishes only within boundaries already established. The appearance of living creatures on Days 5 and 6 confirms that creation is governed by appointment, kind, and realm, not by randomness or self-organization.

The goal of Week 35 is coherence.

Students must be able to trace life's emergence without collapsing structure into biology or stewardship into dominance.

Governing Scriptural Anchors

(Chapters 5–6 — The Three Humanities, Book 1)

The following texts function as juridical anchors, fixing life within prior order:

- Berēshīth (Genesis) 1:20–23 — life fills water and sky by command
- Berēshīth (Genesis) 1:24–25 — land life appears in ordered categories
- Berēshīth (Genesis) 2:7 — human life animated by divine breath, not matter alone
- Qoheleth (Ecclesiastes) 7:29 — humanity created upright
- Iyôb (Job) 40–41 — dominion over Leviathan and Behemoth belongs to Yahuah

Together, these texts establish life as a placed reality, governed by kind, boundary, and blessing.

Teaching Explanation

Chapters 5 and 6 train the student to read creation as a governance sequence.

The interpretive pattern is consistent:

- Realms are formed before they are filled
- Life is introduced by command, not process
- Kinds preserve order
- Dominion remains with Yahuah even where humanity cannot reach

Day 5 introduces nephesh chayah—fleshly, breathing life—only after light, boundaries, land, vegetation, and timekeeping are complete. This sequencing prohibits reading life as self-generating or accidental.

Day 6 (Part 1) extends this logic to the land: creatures are introduced in categories, crowned by Behemoth as a visible witness that the greatest powers of the earth remain created, bounded, and subordinate.
Life does not invent order; it inhabits it.

Life Within Order, Not Origin of Order

Within Yada Yahuah, life is never treated as autonomous.

Scripture assigns:

- waters their creatures
- sky its flyers
- land its beasts
- each realm its limits

The presence of Leviathan and Behemoth serves a juridical purpose:
they testify that human inability does not equal absence of governance.

Where humanity cannot rule, Yahuah already does.

This reading prevents later interpretive error, where power, size, or mystery are mistaken for rebellion or chaos.

Alignment Focus — Chapters 5–6 (Life Within Order)

By the end of Week 35, students must retain the following interpretive conclusions:

- Filling always follows forming
- Nephesh life is introduced by divine command, not material inevitability
- Kinds preserve biological and covenantal order
- Leviathan and Behemoth function as witnesses of Yahuah's dominion
- Human stewardship presupposes a completed, governed world

These are reading controls, not zoological claims.

KEY TERMS — WEEK 35

- Nephesh Chayah
  Fleshly, breathing life introduced by Yahuah's command.
- Kind
  A divinely fixed boundary preserving order and reproduction.
- Stewardship
  Responsible governance exercised within Yahuah's established order.

COVENANTAL STUDY TASK

Using Scripture and Chapters 5–6 only:

•*Explain why Day 5 cannot precede the formation of realms*
•*Demonstrate how "after its kind" functions as an ordering principle*
•*Identify how Leviathan and Behemoth prevent
human-centered readings of dominion*
•*Articulate why humanity's placement at the
end implies stewardship, not authorship*

Remain sequential. Do not import later corruption themes.

FINAL THOUGHTS — WEEK 35

Humanity does not arrive to define creation.

Humanity arrives to administer what has already been defined.

Life exists because order was spoken first.

QUOTE REFLECTION

"Life flourishes where order has already been assigned."

TERM III · MONTH 1 — WEEK 36
SHABBÂTH AND THE PERFECT WORK OF YAHUAH
Completion, Not Fatigue

PURPOSE OF WEEK 36

Chapters 7 and 8 are read this week to establish how The Three Humanities™ requires the student to interpret the seventh day: not as recovery, but as sanctified testimony that creation is finished and that time itself is set apart by covenant order.

This week corrects a recurring Yada Yahuah error: reading Shabbâth as a response to limitation. Scripture positions Shabbâth as the seal of completion— an interpretive boundary that prevents students from attributing later corruption to unfinished creation.

The goal is coherence: students must learn to read Shabbâth as completion declared, not "work continued," and as sanctification of time, not exhaustion.

Governing Scriptural Anchors
(Chapters 7–8 — The Three Humanities, Book 1)

These texts govern interpretation and must be treated as controlling:
- Bereshith 2:1–3 — "finished," "ended," "blessed," "sanctified"
- Shemoth (Exodus) 20:11 — Shabbâth as memorial of completed creation
- Êber (Hebrews) 4:3–4 — rest is entered because works are already finished
- Yôbêl (Jubilees) 2:16–18 — completion by the sixth day; Shabbâth as a great sign; heavenly participation
- Yôbêl 2:23–24 — 22 works aligned with 22 heads for sanctification and blessing
- Yôbêl 2:30–33 — Shabbâth's supremacy among sacred times; enduring testimony

These anchors establish finality, sanctification, and covenantal structure.

Teaching Explanation

Chapters 7–8 must be read with one governing method:

Interpret by sequence: completion precedes sanctification; sanctification interprets what follows.

Read "Rest" as Cessation of Creation, Not Relief from Labor

Your task is to identify how Scripture defines "rest" by its immediate context:

What is stated as completed before rest is mentioned? (Gen 2:1–2)

What does Êber claim about the status of the works when rest is entered? (Heb 4:3–4)

In Yada Yahuah, "rest" here is a legal conclusion: the work category has ended.

- Treat the Seventh Day as a Covenant Sign Written into Time
- The text requires you to read Shabbâth as:
- blessed and sanctified (Gen 2:3)
- a great sign (Jub 2:17)

Shabbâth is not merely a rhythm; it functions as an embedded witness that time belongs to Yahuah.

- Preserve the Two-Level Frame: Heaven and Earth

Jubilees introduces a required interpretive distinction:

- Shabbâth as practiced in Heaven
- Shabbâth as given on Earth as covenant privilege

Do not collapse heavenly practice into human custom, or human practice into universalized ritual. The text uses Heaven-first order to establish authority and precedence.

- **Apply the 22-Pattern as Structural Alignment, Not Numerology**
  Jubilees links the 22 works and the 22 heads "for sanctification and blessing."

Your responsibility is not to embellish this link, but to read it as a structural claim: creation order and covenant line are intentionally coordinated.

The pattern functions as an interpretive constraint—students must track how completion and sanctification extend beyond "events" into covenant structure.

- Use Shabbâth to Prevent Misattribution of Corruption

Once Shabbâth is read as completion and sanctification, it establishes a boundary:

- Later corruption must be read as intrusion, not design defect.
- Later disorder must be read as violation, not unfinished creation.

Shabbâth is the interpretive seal that preserves the integrity of creation categories.

Alignment Focus — Chapters 7 & 8

By the end of Week 36, students must retain these interpretive conclusions:

- Shabbâth begins after completion; it introduces no new work
- "Rest" is defined by finished works, not fatigue
- Shabbâth is a sanctification of time, not a recovery interval
- Shabbâth operates in a Heaven-first frame, then becomes covenant sign on earth
- The 22-pattern is a structural alignment joining creation order to covenant testimony
- Shabbâth functions as the seal that prevents blaming creation for later intrusion

KEY TERMS — WEEK 36

- **Shabbâth**
  The sanctified seventh day functioning as covenantal testimony of completion.
- **Sanctification**
  Setting apart as holy, complete, and belonging to Yahuah.

- **Completion**
  The declared state of lacking nothing within the creation week sequence.

COVENANTAL STUDY TASK

Using Bereshith 2:1–3, Shemoth 20:11, Êber 4:3–4, and Yôbêl 2:16–33 only:
•Demonstrate why Shabbâth cannot be interpreted as fatigue
•Identify the specific textual markers that establish "completion"
before "sanctification"
•Explain how Shabbâth functions as covenant sign rather than ritual burden
•Show how the Heaven-first frame governs earthbound
Shabbâth practice in the text

Remain text-governed. Do not generalize beyond the assigned anchors.

FINAL THOUGHTS — WEEK 36

Shabbâth is not the pause that follows unfinished work.

It is the seal placed upon finished work.

When read correctly, Shabbâth preserves creation's integrity and forces later corruption

to be interpreted as foreign intrusion rather than original deficiency.

QUOTE REFLECTION

"Shabbâth is the witness that nothing was left undone."

TERM III · MONTH 1 — CORE REINFORCEMENT
THE NON-NEGOTIABLE FOUNDATION OF THE THREE HUMANITIES
Purpose of Core Reinforcement

This Core Reinforcement secures the absolute baseline of Term III.

If any principle below is unstable, all later study collapses.

Month 1 does not explain corruption, rebellion, judgment, Edenic failure, or redemption.

It establishes what creation IS before anything goes wrong.

No student may proceed to Month 2 without internal mastery of this core.

CORE AXIOMS — MONTH 1 (WEEKS 33-36)

These are not themes.

They are governing controls.

1. Divine Order Precedes All Matter (Week 33)

- Creation begins with Yahuah's spoken intention, not material causation
- The invisible precedes the visible
- Meaning precedes manifestation
- Spirit precedes body
- Authority precedes form

Anything interpreted as emerging from chaos, matter, evolution, or randomness is rejected

2. Separation Is Architecture, Not Conflict (Week 34)

- Separation assigns function, jurisdiction, and purpose
- The firmament is structure, not atmosphere
- Boundaries preserve life, time, and clarity
- Mixing realms produces corruption

Separation is a condition of life, not a reaction to sin

3. Life Is Placed Within Established Order (Week 35)

- Yahuah forms realms before He fills them
- Life does not invent order — it inhabits order
- Reproduction "after its kind" is both:
  - biological stability
  - covenant boundary

Any view that treats life as self-organizing or self-defining is rejected

4. Humanity Is Created Within a Finished System (Week 35)

- Humanity is not the origin of meaning
- Humanity enters a prepared, governed, sanctified world
- Stewardship is administration, not authorship

Human purpose is alignment, not reinvention

5. Shabbâth Seals Completion, Not Fatigue (Week 36)

- All 22 works are finished before Shabbâth
- Shabbâth sanctifies time itself
- Nothing in creation lacks correction, evolution, or repair
- Corruption is therefore intrusion, not design

If creation were incomplete, redemption would be incoherent

MASTER CONTROL PRINCIPLE — MONTH 1

Creation is perfect, ordered, bounded, and complete.
Therefore corruption is foreign, intrusive, and illegal.

This principle governs:

- Anthropology
- Judgment
- Redemption
- Messiah
- Restoration

MANDATORY STUDENT ACTION (BEFORE MONTH 2)

Students must:
- Re-read any week where confusion remains
- Eliminate inherited religious assumptions
- Refuse to import:
  - sin-nature
  - corruption
  - judgment
  - rebellion
  - Edenic failure

into Creation Week
- Preserve the creational sequence exactly:

Order → Structure → Filling → Stewardship → Sanctified Completion

Failure to internalize Month 1 requires remediation before advancing.

COVENANTAL WARNING

If Month 1 is misunderstood:

Eden will be misread
- Disobedience will be confused with corruption
- Humanity will be misdefined
- Redemption will be distorted
- Yahusha's mission will be misunderstood

Month 1 is not optional groundwork.

It is the load-bearing foundation of The Three Humanities.

TERM III · MONTH 2
MODULE OVERVIEW
The Three Humanities™ — Transition from Creation to Humanity

CHAPTER 9 AS THE GATE · BOOK 2 AS THE FIELD

Term III · Month 2 continues the pinnacle study of The Three Humanities™ by moving from creation order (Month 1) into human existence within that completed order. This transition is governed first by Chapter 9 (Book 1), which seals the 22 Works of Creation as finished, perfected, and sanctified. No study of humanity is permitted until this completion is firmly established.

Only after creation is confirmed as whole does the curriculum proceed into Book 2, beginning with **The First Humanity (Y+A=FH) —**
Yahuah → Adam = The First Humanity (Spirit-first, pure, incorruptible origin).

Month 2 does not begin with corruption.
It begins with alignment.
This module examines humanity as it existed within Edenic order, before hybrid corruption, before the emergence of **The Second Humanity (AW + HW = N & NM + PW = N),** and before the division of mankind through altered flesh.
Using Yada Yahuah, Month 2 addresses purity, authority, deception, disobedience, awareness, and restriction of access without collapsing these events into later doctrines of corruption, inherited guilt, or total depravity.

This month is not about corruption in its final form.
It is about loss of position, loss of access, and the beginning of vulnerability—while humanity remains fully human.

By the end of this month, the student must understand that:

• The First Humanity **(Y+A=FH)** was qadosh, aligned, and complete, yet not immutable

• Humanity existed in two conditions, not two creations

• Disobedience entered through deception, not necessity or force

• The Nachash operated through half-truth, not denial of Yahuah

• "Like one of Us" marks a shift in awareness, not divinity or corruption

• Expulsion from Eden was removal from access, not annihilation of humanity

Month 2 explains how humanity fell from alignment without ceasing to be human, and how redemption begins inside judgment, not after it.

CHAPTER COVERAGE

Week 37 — The First Humanity

> •**Book 1, Chapter 9** — The Perfect Work of Yahuah Êlôhîym — His 22 Works, His 7 Days, His Eternal Seal
>
> •**Book 2, Chapter 1** — The First Humanity (Y+A=FH)

Week 38 — The Two Kinds of Humanity

> •**Book 2, Chapter 2** — The Two Kinds of Humanity
>
> •**Book 2, Chapter 3** — The Origin of Disobedience

Week 39 — Deception and Awareness

> •**Book 2, Chapter 4** — The Half-Truth of the Nachash
>
> •**Book 2, Chapter 5** — "Like One of Us": Knowledge, Not Corruption

Week 40 — Restriction, Mercy, and Separation

> •**Book 2, Chapter 6** — The Expulsion from Eden: The First Act of Mercy
>
> •**Book 2, Chapter 7** — The Separation of Light and Darkness Among Men

GOVERNING INTERPRETIVE RULE — MONTH 2

Creation is complete before humanity's story unfolds.

Therefore, Eden must be read as:

alignment → deception → disobedience → awareness → restricted access

—not as corruption, degeneration, or loss of created identity.

TERM III · MONTH 2 — WEEK 37
THE FIRST HUMANITY (Y+A=FH)
Humanity Within Divine Alignment
(Spirit-first, pure, incorruptible origin)

PURPOSE OF WEEK 37

Week 37 establishes the interpretive baseline for understanding The First Humanity **(Y+A=FH)** as Scripture presents it: qadosh, aligned, and functioning within a completed creation order.

This week does not investigate corruption, transgression, or consequence. Its sole function is to discipline the student's reading posture so that Yahuah → Adam = The First Humanity is interpreted from creation forward, not from later disruption backward.

Chapter 9 closes the creation record as complete and sealed.
Book 2 · Chapter 1 opens human history inside that completed order.
The student must therefore learn to read humanity as placed, not tested; aligned, not deficient; responsible, not remember-fallen.
Failure to maintain this posture results in misreading every later chapter in The Three Humanities.

Governing Scriptural Anchors
(Chapter 9 + Book 2 · Chapter 1)

- Berēshīṯh (Genesis) 1:26–28 — Humanity created with image, authority, and assignment
- Berēshīṯh (Genesis) 2:8–15 — Eden prepared before human placement
- Qoheleth (Ecclesiastes) 7:29 — Humanity made upright
- Yôbêl (Jubilees) 2:16 — All works finished before Shabbâth
- Yôbêl (Jubilees) 3 — Chronology of humanity before corruption

These texts govern interpretation. No later passages may be imported.

Teaching Explanation
Humanity Must Be Read From Completion, Not Collapse

Chapter 9 establishes a non-negotiable rule:
creation is finished, ordered, and sanctified before human history begins.

Therefore, Book 2 · Chapter 1 must be read with this constraint:
- Humanity does not emerge into uncertainty
- Humanity does not awaken into moral instability
- Humanity does not begin in danger or lack

Yahuah → Adam = The First Humanity is introduced inside a perfected system governed by boundaries, time, provision, authority, and Shabbâth.

The student must learn to interpret humanity without assuming failure, because Scripture does not.

The First Humanity Is a Category, Not a Moral Argument
Book 2 · Chapter 1 introduces Yahuah → Adam = The First Humanity as a defined state of existence, not an abstract ideal.

When reading, the student must distinguish between:
- State (qadosh, aligned, instructed)
- Later action (disobedience, intrusion, corruption)

Week 37 trains the student to separate identity from later violation.
Adam and Chawwah are not "good until bad happens."
They are good because creation is good.

Chronology Matters More Than Assumption
Jubilees restores sequence where compression has caused confusion.
The student must read carefully and note:
- Spirits precede bodies
- Bodies precede union
- Union precedes temptation

- Instruction precedes choice

This sequence is not narrative detail — it is juridical order.

Responsibility only exists where instruction and alignment already stand.

Eden Is Context, Not Test

Week 37 requires the student to abandon the assumption that Eden exists primarily as a testing chamber.

Scripture presents Eden as:
- prepared before humanity
- provisioned before labor
- ordered before command
- governed before choice

Testing belongs to later intrusion.

Eden belongs to alignment.

ALIGNMENT FOCUS — CHAPTER 9 + BOOK 2 · CHAPTER 1

By the end of Week 37, the student must be able to retain these anchors:
- Creation is complete before humanity acts
- Humanity begins qadosh, not neutral
- Authority is assigned, not seized
- Alignment is the default state of man
- Responsibility exists because order already exists

These are not conclusions — they are reading controls.

KEY TERMS — WEEK 37

- **The First Humanity**
  Yahuah → Adam = The First Humanity
  (Spirit-first, pure, incorruptible origin)
- **Alignment**
  Harmony between human action and divine instruction within established order.

- **Qadosh**
  Set apart by design, not achieved through recovery.

COVENANTAL STUDY TASK
Using only the governing Scriptures and the assigned chapters:
- *Identify markers that confirm humanity begins upright*
- *Explain why Eden must be read as provision, not probation*
- *Demonstrate how completion of creation limits interpretation of humanity*
- *Describe how instruction precedes accountability*

Do not speculate.
Do not anticipate corruption.
Remain inside the text.

FINAL THOUGHTS — WEEK 37

Humanity does not begin broken.

Humanity begins aligned.

Creation does not explain failure.

Creation exposes failure as foreign.

Only when Yahuah Adam = The First Humanity is understood correctly can the later

humanities be read without distortion.

QUOTE REFLECTION

"Responsibility only exists where order already stands."

"Purity is alignment, not ignorance."

TERM III· MONTH 2 — WEEK 38
THE TWO KINDS OF HUMANITY
Condition, Not Species

PURPOSE OF WEEK 38

Week 38 establishes a decisive interpretive rule within Master-level Yada Yahuah:

Scripture does not divide humanity by race, biology, or origin — but by condition.

This week trains students to read Scripture without collapsing categories, especially the error of projecting later corruption backward into creation or the fall. Students learn to distinguish:

- Creation vs. corruption
- Disobedience vs. alteration of nature
- Condition vs. species

This week depends entirely on disciplined reading of The Three Humanities — Book 2, Chapters 2–3, and must be mastered before progressing.

Governing Texts for Interpretation

Students are not asked what these texts say, but what distinctions they establish.

- Bereshith (Genesis) 1:26–27
  Humanity created in image, authority, and alignment
- Bereshith (Genesis) 3:22
  Knowledge acquired, not nature altered
- Qoheleth (Ecclesiastes) 7:29
  Humanity made upright at origin
- Sefer Yôbêl (Jubilees) 3–4
  Preservation after Eden; delayed corruption
- 1 Corinthians 15:45–49
  Distinction between spirit-governed and flesh-governed humanity

Primary Doctrinal Source

The Three Humanities — Book 2

- Chapter 2: The Two Kinds of Humanity
- Chapter 3: The Origin of Disobedience

Interpretive Framework — What Students Must Learn to See

- Humanity Is Divided by Condition, Not Creation

At first mention only:

The First Humanity (Y+A=FH) (Spirit-first, pure, incorruptible origin)

There is one creation of humanity, not two. Scripture never presents multiple human species. Instead, it reveals two conditions of humanity emerging at different stages of history.

Students must learn to ask:

- What changed?
- When did it change?
- What did not change?

Failure here produces category collapse and misreading of Scripture.

Disobedience Does Not Equal Corruption

Chapter 3 establishes a non-negotiable distinction in Yada Yahuah:

- Disobedience = violation of command
- Corruption = alteration of nature

Eating from the Tree introduces awareness, not decay.

Knowledge is gained; purity is not lost.

Students must demonstrate from Scripture alone that:

- No genetic corruption appears in Eden
- No demonic activity appears in Eden
- No sickness or decay begins immediately
- Humanity remains aligned with the Ruach

This confirms continued identity as:

Yahuah → Adam = The First Humanity

(Spirit-first, pure, incorruptible origin)

Preservation After Eden Is Intentional

A core interpretive discipline of Week 38:

Yahuah preserves humanity long after Eden.

For nearly 1,200 years, Scripture records:

- Extraordinary longevity
- Absence of disease
- Continued worship
- No demonic oppression
- No hybrid corruption

Students must recognize preservation as intentional restraint, not delay or ignorance.

The Second Humanity Is Introduced, Not Assumed:

The Second Humanity (AW + HW = N & NM + PW = N)

Meaning:

1. Angels Watchers + Human Women = Nephilim

2. Nephilim Men + Pure Women = More Nephilim

Scripture places the true shift not at Eden, but in the days of Yârêd.

Only when:

- Watchers abandon their appointed nature
- Unlawful unions occur
- Hybrid offspring are born

...does a new human condition emerge.

This condition is:

- Flesh-driven
- Altered
- Violent

- Spiritually disordered

Students must learn to identify where Scripture marks transition, rather than importing assumptions.

Why This Distinction Is Redemptively Necessary

If corruption begins in Eden:

- Creation is flawed
- Yahuah's work is incomplete
- Shabbâth testifies falsely

If corruption begins later:

- Creation remains perfect
- Judgment is just .
- Restoration restores, not repairs

Week 38 protects the integrity of:

- Creation order
- Judgment sequence
- Redemption alignment

KEY TERMS (WEEK 38)

- **Two Kinds of Humanity**

  Two spiritual conditions of human existence, not two creations

- **The First Humanity (Y+A=FH)**

  Yahuah → Adam = The First Humanity

  (Spirit-first, pure, incorruptible origin)

- **The Second Humanity (AW + HW = N & NM + PW = N)**

  Humanity altered through corruption introduced by Watcher rebellion

- **Condition**

  The internal spiritual and biological state shaping human existence

- **Preservation**

  Yahuah's restraint of corruption until the appointed time

COVENANTAL STUDY TASK
Using Book 2, Chapters 2–3 only:
• Explain the difference between kind and condition
• Identify why Eden introduces awareness but not corruption
• Demonstrate from Scripture when the Second Humanity begins
• Defend why humanity remains preserved after Eden
No external frameworks. No inherited assumptions.

FINAL THOUGHTS — WEEK 38

"Humanity changed condition, not creation."

The fall altered awareness.

Corruption altered nature.

Scripture never confuses the two.

QUOTE REFLECTION

"A fall alters position, not origin."

THE ORIGIN OF DISOBEDIENCE & THE HALF-TRUTH OF THE NACHASH

Deception as the Doorway

PURPOSE OF WEEK 39

Week 39 establishes a non-negotiable interpretive boundary within Master-level Yada Yahuah:

Disobedience is not corruption.

Students are trained to read Eden without importing later categories of genetic alteration, spiritual contamination, or inherited corruption. This week focuses on how deception functions, how authority is reframed rather than denied, and how judgment immediately contains redemption.

Failure to master this distinction collapses creation order, misrepresents divine justice, and distorts the necessity and timing of redemption.

Governing Scriptural Anchors

Students must identify how these texts function, not merely what they report.

- Bereshith (Genesis) 3:1–5
  Deception operates through distortion and selective framing
- Yochanan (John) 8:44
  Falsehood imitates truth to gain trust
- 2 Corinthians 11:3
  Corruption of the mind occurs through subtle deception, not force

These texts establish deception as cognitive and relational, not coercive or transformational.

Primary Doctrinal Source

The Three Humanities — Book 2

- Chapter 4: The Half-Truth of the Nachash
- Chapter 5: "Like One of Us": Knowledge, Not Corruption

Students must remain confined to these chapters when forming conclusions.

Interpretive Training — How to Read This Section Correctly

Deception Works by Reframing Authority, Not Denying It

Students must observe that the Nachash does not:

- Deny Yahuah exists
- Deny Yahuah spoke
- Deny consequence exists

Instead, he reframes timing and outcome.

This establishes a core rule of Yada Yahuah interpretation:

The most dangerous deception affirms authority while altering trust.

A Half-Truth Is More Effective Than a Lie

Chapter 4 trains students to identify partial accuracy paired with concealed consequence.

Interpretive discipline required:

- Separate what is factually accurate
- From what is strategically omitted

The Nachash speaks what appears true in the immediate frame while concealing Yahuah's temporal scale and redemptive intent.

"In the Day You Eat" Must Be Read by Divine Measure

Students must be trained to:

- Reject human time assumptions
- Apply Scriptural definitions of Yahuah's "day"

Chapter 4 demonstrates that:

- Judgment is exact
- Fulfillment is precise
- Yahuah's word is neither exaggerated nor delayed

This preserves Scriptural integrity and prevents accusations of false warning or unjust judgment.

Knowledge Introduces Awareness, Not Alteration of Nature

Chapter 5 establishes a decisive interpretive distinction:

- Knowledge does not equal corruption
- Awareness does not equal defilement

Students must learn to separate:

- Change of condition
- From change of created nature

The phrase "like one of Us" must be read as relational (yada), not moral or essential.

Judgment Immediately Serves Redemption

A key reading skill taught this week:

Never read judgment without tracing its redemptive function.

Students must identify how:

- Mortality limits rebellion
- Exile prevents eternal corruption
- Boundaries create future restoration

This trains students to see redemption as embedded, not reactive.

ALIGNMENT FOCUS — CHAPTERS 4 & 5

Students must extract and retain these anchors:

- Disobedience violates command but does not redefine humanity
- The Nachash operates through half-truth, not denial
- Death is fulfilled precisely within Yahuah's time
- Mortality is a redemptive boundary
- Knowledge alters awareness, not essence
- The image of Elohiym remains intact
- Redemption begins immediately, not after compounded failure

KEY TERMS (WEEK 39)

- Disobedience
  Violation of divine instruction without alteration of created nature

- Nachash
  The deceiving agent who reframes truth through distortion
- Half-Truth
  Partial accuracy designed to obscure consequence
- Awareness
  Moral perception gained without participation in evil

COVENANTAL STUDY TASK

Using Chapters 4–5 only, students must:

•Identify the exact half-truth spoken by the Nachash
•Explain why the deception succeeded
without denying Yahuah
•Distinguish awareness, disobedience,
and corruption from Scripture
•Demonstrate how judgment simultaneously
limits corruption and enables redemption

No inherited assumptions. No external systems.

FINAL THOUGHTS — WEEK 39

Disobedience does not redefine creation.

Awareness does not corrupt nature.

Judgment does not abandon redemption.

Creation remains intact.

Redemption is already moving.

QUOTE REFLECTION

"Deception succeeds when truth is reframed."

TERM III · MONTH 2 — WEEK 40
"LIKE ONE OF US" & THE EXPULSION FROM EDEN
Loss of Access, Not Loss of Humanity

PURPOSE OF WEEK 40

This week establishes a decisive interpretive boundary in Yada Yahuah:
Disobedience alters access and condition — not humanity itself.

Scripture does not teach that Adam and Chawwâh lost identity, image, or created status after Eden. Instead, Yahuah restricts access to immortality as an act of mercy, ensuring redemption remains possible.

Week 40 teaches students how to read Bereshith 3 without importing later corruption frameworks, and how to recognize the expulsion from Eden as the first redemptive boundary, not punitive rejection.

Read and Instruction

- Bereshith (Genesis) 3:22–24
  Humanity gains awareness but is barred from the Tree of Life to prevent eternal disobedience.
- Yasha'yahu (Isaiah) 59:1–2
  Separation occurs, yet Yahuah's power and intention to save remain unchanged.
- Êber (Hebrews) 9:27
  Mortality is the appointed boundary enabling judgment and redemption.

Alignment Focus — The Three Humanities (Chapters 6 & 7)
Students are to extract the following interpretive anchors, not narrative detail:

"Like One of Us" Refers to Knowledge, Not Corruption
Bereshith defines the change explicitly: knowledge of good and evil.
- Awareness increases

- Moral consciousness awakens
- Accountability begins

Nothing in the text states corruption of nature, loss of image, or spiritual destruction.

In Yada Yahuah, awareness does not equal corruption.

Humanity Remains the First Humanity (Y + A = FH)
(Yahuah + Adam = The First Humanity — spirit-first, pure, incorruptible origin)

After Eden, humanity remains:
- Image-bearing
- Spirit-capable
- Instruction-receiving
- Longevity-retaining
- Fellowship-maintaining

In interpretive terms: Yahuah → Adam = The First Humanity
(condition changed, origin intact)

Expulsion Is Protective Mercy, Not Punishment

Yahuah's concern in Bereshith 3:22 is explicit:

"Lest he take also of the Tree of Life and live forever..."

Immortality after disobedience would mean:
- Eternal rebellion
- Irredeemable humanity
- No Messiah
- No resurrection

The expulsion protects humanity from permanent ruin and preserves the possibility of restoration.

Mortality Is a Redemptive Boundary

Death is introduced not as abandonment, but as containment.

Mortality:
- Prevents eternal corruption
- Makes resurrection possible
- Creates space for Messiah
- Preserves humanity for renewal

In Yada Yahuah, death is not the enemy of redemption — it is its doorway.

Separation of Light and Darkness Begins Historically — Not in Eden
For nearly 1,000 years after Eden, humanity remains aligned with Yahuah.

Only later does true corruption appear with The Second Humanity (AW + HW = N & NM + PW = N)
(Angels/Watchers + Human Women = Nephilim; Nephilim Men + Pure Women = more Nephilim)

This marks:
- Genetic alteration
- Flesh corruption
- Violence and sorcery
- The real division between light and darkness

Eden introduces awareness.
The Watchers introduce corruption.

Teaching Explanation
Week 40 trains students to read Scripture sequentially and lawfully.
- Adam becomes "like one of Us" in knowledge, not rebellion
- Humanity loses access, not identity
- Eden closes so redemption can open
- Separation is preservation, not rejection

The expulsion from Eden is the first deliberate redemptive act in history.

Key Terms and Definitions (Week 40)

- Awareness

  Moral knowledge gained without alteration of created nature.

- Expulsion

  Protective restriction of access to prevent eternal corruption.

- Tree of Life

  The source of sustained immortality, withheld to preserve redemption.

COVENANTAL STUDY TASK

Before proceeding, students must:

•Explain why immortality after disobedience would nullify redemption

•Distinguish awareness, condition, and corruption using Bereshith 3

•Identify where corruption actually begins in history

Responses must remain within Scripture and The Three Humanities. Philosophical or inherited doctrinal assumptions are not permitted.

FINAL THOUGHTS — WEEK 40

Loss of access is not loss of humanity.

Eden was closed so salvation could proceed.

Yahuah removed humanity from danger — not from purpose.

QUOTE REFLECTION

"Yahuah barred immortality to preserve redemption."

"Mercy sometimes looks like exile."

TERM III · MONTH 2 — CORE REINFORCEMENT (WEEKS 37–40)
PURPOSE

This section reinforces the non-negotiable interpretive boundaries of Month 2. If any principle below is unclear, the student must return to the corresponding week before proceeding to Month 3.

Month 2 governs how humanity moves from alignment to vulnerability without corruption, and how redemption begins inside judgment, not after history collapses.

Creation Is the Governing Context of Humanity (Week 37)

- Humanity is introduced only after creation is completed, sealed, and sanctified
- Chapter 9 (Book 1) governs all anthropology in Book 2
- Humanity does not emerge into chaos, testing, or uncertainty
- The First Humanity (Y+A=FH) enters a world already ordered, bounded, illuminated, and complete

Interpretive Boundary:

Humanity never explains creation; creation explains humanity.

The First Humanity Exists in Alignment, Not Fragility (Week 37)

- The First Humanity (Y+A=FH) is spirit-first, pure, and incorruptible in origin
- Purity does not mean ignorance; it means alignment
- Authority is granted, not seized
- Fellowship precedes command, not the reverse

Interpretive Boundary:

Humanity was created whole, not probationary.

Humanity Is Divided by Condition, Not by Creation (Week 38)

- Scripture presents two kinds of humanity, defined by spiritual condition

- Disobedience does not create a new humanity
- Corruption does not begin in Eden
- The First Humanity continues for centuries after Eden

Interpretive Boundary:

Difference in condition does not equal difference in creation.

Disobedience Is Not Corruption (Week 38–39)

- Disobedience introduces violation of instruction, not alteration of nature
- Adam and Chawwâh gain awareness, not wickedness
- The image (tzelem) of Elohiym is retained
- Longevity, alignment, and fellowship continue

Interpretive Boundary:

Breaking a command does not rewrite creation.

The Nachash Operates Through Half-Truth, Not Denial (Week 39)

- The Nachash does not deny Yahuah's word
- He reframes timing and conceals consequence
- Deception succeeds by partial truth, not open rebellion
- Trust is redirected, not destroyed

Interpretive Boundary:

Deception corrupts understanding before it ever corrupts behavior.

"Like One of Us" Refers to Knowledge, Not Corruption (Week 39–40)

- Humanity becomes like Yahuah in knowing, not in divinity or rebellion
- Awareness does not equal participation
- Knowledge of evil does not implant evil
- Condition changes; essence does not

Interpretive Boundary:

Awareness alters responsibility, not identity.

Expulsion from Eden Is Protective Mercy (Week 40)

- Humanity is removed from access, not from covenant purpose
- The Tree of Life is restricted to prevent eternal rebellion
- Mortality becomes the gateway to resurrection
- Redemption begins immediately within judgment

Interpretive Boundary:

Loss of access is not loss of humanity.

CUMULATIVE MONTH 2 MASTER PRINCIPLE

Humanity fell from alignment, not from creation.

Awareness entered without corruption.

Judgment arrived carrying mercy.

Redemption began before history advanced

MANDATORY STUDENT ACTION (BEFORE MONTH 3)

•Re-read any week where disobedience and corruption are confused

•Do not import Watcher corruption, hybridization, or judgment themes into Eden

•Preserve the sequence:

creation → alignment → deception → disobedience → awareness → restricted access → redemption

Failure to hold this sequence invalidates later study of corruption, judgment, and restoration.

TERM III · MONTH 2 — MASTER-LEVEL ESSAY

Pinnacle Assessment · Eden, Alignment, and Awareness

Length: 1,500–2,000 words

Status: REQUIRED

Essay Prompt — Month 2

Explain how Scripture presents The First Humanity (Yahuah → Adam = The First Humanity) as aligned, qadosh, and fully human within a completed creation order, and demonstrate why Eden must be interpreted as a context of alignment rather than probation.

Your essay must:

- Demonstrate why creation completion (Chapter 9, Book 1) governs all interpretation of humanity in Book 2
- Distinguish clearly between:
    - alignment and obedience
    - disobedience and corruption
    - awareness and alteration of nature
- Explain how the Nachash operates through half-truth, reframing authority without denying Yahuah
- Analyze the phrase "like one of Us" as a shift in knowledge and accountability, not divinity or corruption
- Defend why expulsion from Eden functions as protective mercy, preserving redemption rather than terminating humanity
- Preserve the required sequence:

    creation → alignment → deception → disobedience → awareness → restricted access → redemption

Constraints

- Use Scripture and The Three Humanities (Book 2) only
- Do not import:
    - inherited guilt
    - total depravity
    - genetic corruption
    - Watcher rebellion
- Maintain strict Yada' Yahuah discipline: no philosophical, theological, or denominational overlays

Evaluation Criteria

- Scriptural accuracy and sequence control
- Category precision (alignment vs. corruption)
- Faithful use of defined terminology
- Logical coherence without doctrinal projection
- Demonstrated mastery of Eden as loss of access, not loss of humanity

TERM III · MONTH 3
MODULE OVERVIEW
The Three Humanities™ — Book 2 & Book 3 (Transition Module)

Preservation, Prophetic Purpose, and the Emergence of Corruption
Term III · Month 3 completes the formal study of *The First Humanity (Yahuah → Adam = The First Humanity) and initiates the controlled transition into The Second Humanity (AW + HW = N & NM + PW = N).*

This month does not revisit Eden, creation order, or the loss of access already established in prior months. Instead, it examines what Scripture emphasizes next: preservation, separation, lineage, purity under pressure, and prophetic preparation before open conflict.

Scripture does not present the period between Eden and the Flood as morally undefined or spiritually collapsed. Rather, it documents an extended era in which alignment is guarded, purity is preserved, and covenant memory is intentionally maintained, even as external conditions deteriorate.

This month trains students to interpret Scripture through Yada Yahuah by learning to:
- Track alignment instead of population
- Read genealogy as covenant architecture
- Distinguish vulnerability from corruption
- Identify preparation before judgment
- Recognize that redemption is protected before it is required

Term III · Month 3 establishes the necessary interpretive framework for understanding why corruption later becomes catastrophic, why judgment is decisive, and why preservation precedes cleansing.

By the end of this month, the student will be able to demonstrate that:

- Light and darkness function as covenant states, not metaphors
- Purity exists after Eden and before corruption
- Lineage is preserved intentionally, not accidentally
- Prophetic purpose precedes historical crisis
- The emergence of The Second Humanity (AW + HW = N & NM + PW = N) is an intrusion, not a development

This module forms the bridge between preserved humanity and open corruption.

CHAPTER COVERAGE

The Three Humanities™ — Structured Weekly Alignment
Each instructional week is anchored to exactly two chapters, and weeks function as interpretive training, not chapter repetition.

Week 41

Book 2 — *The First Humanity (Yahuah → Adam = The First Humanity)*

- Chapter 8 — The Patriarchal Line of the First Humanity (Yahuah → Adam = The First Humanity)
- Chapter 9 — The Purity of the First Humanity (Yahuah → Adam = The First Humanity) Before the Flood

Focus:

Lineage as covenant continuity; purity preserved under increasing vulnerability.

Week 42

Book 2 — The First Humanity (Y+A=FH)

- Chapter 10 — The Prophetic Purpose of the First Humanity (Yahuah → Adam = The First Humanity)
- Chapter 11 — The Hidden Preparation for the Coming Conflict

Focus:

Prophetic design, covenant memory, and preparation before crisis.

Week 43

Book 3 — The Second Humanity (AW + HW = N & NM + PW = N)

- *Chapter 1 — The Nature of the Second Humanity*
  (AW + HW = N & NM + PW = N)
- *Chapter 2 — The Inheritance of the Second Humanity*
  (AW + HW = N & NM + PW = N)

Focus:

The emergence of The Second Humanity *(AW + HW = N & NM + PW = N)* as a corrupt intrusion lacking the Ruach.

Week 44

Book 3 — The Second Humanity (AW + HW = N & NM + PW = N)

- Chapter 3 — Why the Second Humanity (AW + HW = N & NM + PW = N) Has No Redemption
- Chapter 4 — The Mercy of Yahuah Amid Rising Corruption

Focus:

Non-redeemability of the hybrid line and the preservation of Noach as the final uncorrupted carrier of Adam's Ruach.

MODULE OUTCOME — TERM III · MONTH 3

Mastery is demonstrated when the student can:

- Interpret Scripture without projecting later corruption backward
- Maintain categorical precision between purity, vulnerability, and corruption
- Trace covenant continuity through preserved lineage
- Recognize preparation as evidence of divine foresight
- Transition accurately from The First Humanity (Yahuah → Adam = The First Humanity) to The Second Humanity *(AW + HW = N & NM + PW = N)* without doctrinal collapse

TERM III · MONTH 3
WEEK 41 — THE SEPARATION OF LIGHT AND DARKNESS
Moral and Covenant Distinction

PURPOSE OF WEEK 41

This week trains the student to identify how Scripture signals separation after Eden without invoking corruption, genetic alteration, or species division. Scripture does not narrate early humanity by population growth, technological development, or cultural achievement. Instead, it records alignment, departure, and preservation. Week 41 establishes how light and darkness first appear among humanity as covenantal orientations—modes of recognition and allegiance—rather than as abstract principles

This interpretive framework is essential. Without it, students will misread genealogy, judgment, and redemption as moral commentary rather than structural continuity of light.

READ AND INSTRUCTION

Students must read the following passages with interpretive intent, not as narrative history or devotional material. Each passage is assigned to train the student to recognize alignment shifts, covenantal separation, and textual signaling, as taught in The Three Humanities.

- Bereshith (Genesis) 4:1–16
  The First Recorded Divergence of Alignment

This passage must be read as the first visible divergence within a single human family, not as the origin of corruption or the emergence of a new humanity.

Students are to observe:

- How obedience and trust are contrasted with self-assertion and resentment
- That Yahuah addresses Cain before judgment, offering correction
- That Cain's defining action is departure from the Presence, not biological change

- That Scripture tracks relational orientation, not moral totality

This text trains the student to recognize movement away from light without importing later categories of corruption or hybridization.

- Bereshith (Genesis) 4:25–26
  Textual Marker of Re-Alignment and Preservation
- This passage must be read as a covenantal signal, not a genealogical footnote.
- Students are to identify:
- That the birth of Seth represents restoration of alignment, not replacement of humanity
- That "calling upon the Name of Yahuah" signals intentional re-orientation toward divine authority

That Scripture begins to track lineage for preservation, not demographic reporting

This passage teaches how Scripture marks light continuity through selective focus.

2 Corinthians 6:14–18
- Apostolic Confirmation of Covenant Incompatibility
  This passage must be read as a New Covenant confirmation of an ancient principle, not a reinterpretation of Genesis.

Students are to observe:
- That light and darkness are defined as incompatible covenant states, not moral degrees
- That separation functions as preservation, not condemnation
- That Paul's language mirrors the same alignment logic present in early Genesis

This passage confirms that separation is not a later invention, but a consistent divine pattern.

INSTRUCTIONAL BOUNDARY

Students must not:

- Treat these passages as isolated moral lessons
- Import post-Flood, post-Torah, or post-Messiah assumptions
- Collapse separation into corruption or racial division

Students must:

- Observe textual movement
- Track alignment and departure
- Apply the interpretive discipline established in The Three Humanities

Teaching Explanation

- Separation Responds to Vulnerability, Not Immediate Corruption
  After Eden, humanity does not immediately enter corruption. Instead,
  Scripture records a prolonged period of moral vulnerability within intact
  created order. Early signs—jealousy, rivalry, resentment, fear—affect
  behavior, not nature.

Yahuah responds not by destroying humanity, but by marking, instructing,
and separating. Separation emerges as a protective architecture, ensuring that
alignment remains traceable.

- **Cain and Abel: Alignment, Not Identity**
  Cain and Abel do not represent two species, bloodlines, or creations. They
  represent two orientations of will within the same humanity.
- Abel remains aligned through trust and obedience
- Cain resists correction and moves away from Presence

Scripture does not redefine Cain's humanity. It records his directional departure.
This pattern becomes foundational:

departure precedes darkness; darkness does not redefine humanity.

- **Seth and the Recovery of Alignment**
  Genesis 4:26 is a structural marker, not narrative filler. The text signals that
  alignment is being intentionally restored and preserved.

Calling upon the Name of Yahuah marks:

- Conscious covenantal orientation
- Communal re-alignment
- The beginning of tracked preservation

From this point forward, Scripture follows light deliberately, not exhaustively.

Light and Darkness as Covenant States

Drawing from The Three Humanities, light and darkness are not abstract moral categories. They are relational states:

- Light: alignment with Yahuah's order, authority, and instruction
- Darkness: departure from that alignment

Paul's teaching confirms this logic. Light and darkness cannot co-govern. Separation becomes necessary to preserve continuity of redemption.

Lineage as Redemptive Architecture

Scripture narrows its focus because redemption requires continuity, not visibility. The patriarchal line is not ancestry alone—it is containment. This prepares the reader for the coming crisis of corruption without misattributing it to Eden or early disobedience.

KEY TERMS AND DEFINITIONS (WEEK 41)

- Light
  Alignment with Yahuah's order, instruction, and covenantal authority.
- Darkness
  Departure from divine alignment while remaining fully human.
- Separation
  A deliberate, redemptive distinction established to preserve purity and continuity.

COVENANTAL STUDY TASK

Students must complete the following:

•*Identify how light and darkness manifest without genetic, racial, or species language*

•*Explain why Scripture tracks separation and lineage rather than population or culture*

•*Demonstrate how separation preserves redemption rather than punishing humanity*

All responses must be text-driven and structurally reasoned.

FINAL THOUGHTS — WEEK 41

"Scripture follows light, not numbers."

Where alignment is preserved, redemption remains possible.

Where separation is maintained, truth remains traceable.

QUOTE REFLECTION

"Where light is preserved, truth remains recoverable."

THE PATRIARCHAL LINE OF THE FIRST HUMANITY (Y+A=FH)

Covenant Continuity

PURPOSE OF WEEK 42

Week 42 trains the student to correctly interpret genealogical structure within the framework of Yada Yahuah.

Scriptural genealogies are not neutral records. They function as alignment markers, preserving covenant continuity under increasing historical pressure. This week establishes how to read genealogies as intentional witnesses of preserved order, rather than as biological, ethnic, or chronological data sets. The student must learn to recognize that Scripture tracks alignment, not population.

READ AND INSTRUCTION

Students must read the following texts before analysis

Bereshith (Genesis) 5:1–24

Students are to observe:

- repetition of relational language,
- emphasis on succession rather than achievement,
- absence of corruption terminology,
- consistency of lifespan reporting as continuity signals.

The interpretive task is to identify what continuity is being preserved, not who lived longest.

Luqas (Luke) 3:23–38

Students must trace:

- backward continuity rather than forward replacement,
- linkage across covenants,
- preservation of identity rather than escalation of status.

The genealogy is functioning as validation, not expansion.

Êber (Hebrews) 11:5

Chanok functions as an

- fellowship with Yahuah is shown to be possible outside Eden,
- translation occurs without death,
- alignment precedes later disruption.

This verse anchors continuity prior to corruption.

Student Textbook Reading

The Three Humanities — Book 2

- Chapter 9
- Chapter 10

Students are not summarizing these chapters.

They are extracting interpretive principles governing lineage, preservation, and purpose.

Interpretive Framework (Yada Yahuah Focus)

Genealogy as Alignment Evidence

Within Yada Yahuah, genealogy functions as ordered testimony.

Scripture uses lineage to demonstrate:

- preserved instruction,
- stable identity,
- uninterrupted transmission of purpose.

Students must reject the assumption that genealogy equals ancestry alone.

It equals continuity of alignment.

Continuity Before Corruption

Chapters 9–10 establish that corruption is not assumed but introduced historically.

Therefore:

- genealogies function as a pre-corruption control structure,
- preservation is demonstrated before judgment is required,
- later disruption is measurable because continuity already existed.

This protects interpretation from projecting later collapse backward.

Transmission vs. Inheritance

Yada Yahuah requires distinction between:

- biological inheritance
- covenantal transmission

The patriarchal line transmits:

- instruction,
- worship practice,
- remembrance,
- relational orientation toward Yahuah.

Alignment is taught, guarded, and modeled, not genetically encoded.

The First Humanity (Y+A=FH) as Reference Standard

The First Humanity (Y+A=FH) functions as the reference condition, not a temporary phase.

All later deviations are measured against this preserved order.

Judgment occurs because alignment was known, modeled, and maintained.

Without this standard, corruption would be undefined.

Redemption as Anchored Continuity

Redemption is not reactive within Yada Yahuah.

Genealogies demonstrate that:

- purpose is preserved before crisis,
- alignment precedes confrontation,
- restoration returns humanity to a known condition, not an abstract ideal.

Continuity anchors restoration.

Alignment Focus — Chapters 9 & 10

Students must extract and articulate:

- Alignment as preserved condition
- Purity as guarded responsibility

- Genealogy as structural witness
- Redemption as pre-embedded purpose
- Continuity across covenantal stages

These are interpretive controls, not doctrinal claims.

KEY TERMS (WEEK 42)

- Patriarchal Line
- A preserved sequence maintaining covenant alignment.
- Genealogy
- A structural record demonstrating continuity of purpose.
- Continuity
- Sustained transmission of instruction and identity.

COVENANTAL STUDY TASK

Students must complete the following analytically:

- **Explain why Scripture records this lineage and excludes others**
- **Demonstrate how alignment is transmitted across generations**
- **Show how genealogy functions as covenantal evidence**

Constraints:

- Use Scripture directly
- No narrative reconstruction
- No later-stage assumptions

FINAL ORIENTATION — WEEK 42

Scripture preserves lineage to preserve order.

Order safeguards purpose.

Purpose enables restoration.

QUOTE REFLECTION

"Continuity is how purpose survives pressure."

THE PURITY OF THE FIRST HUMANITY BEFORE THE FLOOD

Purity Under Pressure

PURPOSE OF WEEK 43

This week trains students to apply Yada Yahuah as an interpretive control when approaching texts that describe both preservation and emerging corruption. The goal is not to determine whether corruption exists, but to teach students how Scripture differentiates preserved humanity from corrupted intrusion without collapsing categories.

Students are taught to recognize a common interpretive failure: treating the appearance of corruption as proof of universal condition.

Week 43 establishes the methodological principle that purity is a definable, traceable state that must be evaluated textually, not assumed retrospectively.

READ AND INSTRUCTION

Students must read the following texts analytically, applying category control and temporal sequencing.

- Primary Scripture
- Bereshith (Genesis) 6:1–8

  Students must identify what the text asserts, what it limits, and what it does not universalize.

- Bereshith (Genesis) 5:28–29

  Observe how continuity is established before evaluative judgment is introduced.

- Enoch 1:1–2

  Determine what the presence of revelation implies about access, alignment, and audience at this stage.

The Three Humanities — Book Three, Chapters 1–2

Students must reference, not reproduce, definitions found there.

Interpretive Training: Yada Yahuah Application

Distinguishing Presence from Dominance

Students must learn to ask:

- Does the text describe existence, increase, or totality?
- Is corruption described as introduced, spreading, or defining all humanity?

Yada Yahuah Rule:

A condition is not universal unless the text removes all distinction.

Category Control: Origin vs. Condition

Week 43 requires students to maintain strict separation between:

- What Yahuah formed
- What rebellion introduced

This is not a moral distinction but a categorical one.

Yada Yahuah Rule:

Do not assign properties of an introduced category to an original one unless the text explicitly merges them.

Evaluative Language Requires a Standard

Students must identify:

- Who is evaluated
- By what measure
- Against what baseline

Judgment language only functions if a preserved reference state exists.

Yada Yahuah Rule:

Judgment presupposes continuity of an evaluative standard.

Temporal Discipline

Students must resist reading later outcomes backward.

Key question:

- Is the text describing a process or a completed condition?

Yada Yahuah Rule:

Later destruction does not define earlier identity.

Alignment Focus — Interpretive Anchors (Week 43)

Students must demonstrate mastery of the following methodological anchors, **not doctrinal conclusions:**

- Purity must be textually identified, not assumed absent
- Corruption must be localized before it can be generalized
- Intrusion does not redefine creation
- Judgment language implies preserved distinction
- Continuity must be disproven, not presumed broken

KEY TERMS WEEK 43

- Purity

  A textually preserved state of alignment identifiable through distinction and continuity.

- Pressure

  The presence of competing conditions without categorical merger.

- Interpretive Collapse

  The error of assigning later-defined conditions to earlier textual states.

-

COVENANTAL STUDY TASK

Students must complete the following:

•Identify where the text maintains distinction rather than collapsing humanity

•Demonstrate how Yada Yahuah prevents retrospective corruption assumptions

•Explain why Scripture can describe increasing darkness without redefining humanity wholesale

All answers must reference textual mechanics, not narrative conclusions.

FINAL INSTRUCTION — WEEK 43

Week 43 does not teach what to believe about pre-Flood humanity.

It teaches how to read the texts without violating their structure.

Yada Yahuah does not permit assumption.

It demands discipline, sequence, and category integrity.

THE PROPHETIC PURPOSE & HIDDEN PREPARATION FOR CONFLICT

Destiny Before Crisis

PURPOSE OF WEEK 44

Week 44 trains the student to read transition texts without collapsing categories, importing later assumptions, or moralizing structural distinctions. The instructional goal is not what happened, but how Scripture signals movement from preservation to confrontation.

This week establishes a governing principle of Yada Yahuah:

Yahuah prepares structurally before He responds historically.

Students are trained to identify pre-crisis markers, not crisis outcomes.

READ AND INSTRUCTION

Students must read the assigned texts as indicators of alignment and capacity, not as narrative events.

Primary Scripture

- Bereshith (Genesis) 6:9
  Observe how Scripture qualifies Noach within generations, not merely as an individual.
- Enoch 10:1–14
  Identify ordered response (containment, separation, preservation) before global judgment.
- Amos 3:7
  Establish the rule that judgment follows revelation, never precedes it.

Student Textbook Reading

The Three Humanities — Book Three

- Chapter 3
- Chapter 4

Students are not to restate these chapters.

They are to extract structural logic governing redemption, capacity, and preservation.

Teaching Explanation

Week 44 teaches the student to distinguish between:

- Corruption within design
- Intrusion outside design

Scripture does not treat all beings equally because capacity is not equal.

When Scripture moves from:

The First Humanity *(Y + A = FH)*

(Yahuah → Adam = Spirit-first humanity)

to

The Second Humanity *(AW + HW = N & NM + PW = N)*

(Angelic Watchers + Human Women = Nephilim; & Nephilim Men + Pure Women = More Nephilim)

it does not describe moral decline —

it marks essential disruption.

This distinction explains:

- why preservation precedes judgment
- why Noach is defined generationally
- why redemption is protected, not expanded

Yada Yahuah reads lineage, breath, and capacity — not sentiment.

Alignment Focus — Interpretive Anchors (Week 44)

From Chapters 3 and 4, students must extract discernment mechanics, not doctrinal conclusions.

- Capacity Determines Redemptive Eligibility

Redemption requires Ruach-bearing continuity, not ethical potential.

- Intrusion does not equal Fall

The Second Humanity *(AW + HW = N & NM + PW = N)* is not a fallen form of The First Humanity *(Y + A = FH)*.

- Preservation Is a Pre-Judgment Act
  Noach is preserved before the Flood narrative escalates.
- Mercy Operates Structurally
  Mercy is not emotional restraint; it is covenantal safeguarding.
- Conflict Activates Existing Design
  Crisis reveals preparation — it does not create it.

KEY TERMS WEEK 44

- Yada Yahuah
  The covenantal act of knowing Yahuah through His self-revelation, instruction, and lived obedience. It is not speculative reasoning about Elohiym, but relational knowing grounded in faithfulness, encounter, and submission to His Word.
- Preservation
  Intentional safeguarding of redemptive continuity prior to confrontation.
- Capacity
  The ability to receive covenant, correction, and restoration.

COVENANTAL STUDY TASK

Students must demonstrate interpretive control by completing the following:

•Explain why redemption cannot be extended without Ruach capacity
•Identify how Scripture marks transition without collapse
•Demonstrate why Noach functions as a structural bridge,
not a moral exception

All responses must remain within Yada Yahuah and assigned texts only.

FINAL INSTRUCTIONAL EMPHASIS — WEEK 44

Week 44 is not about judgment.

It is about how Scripture teaches students to recognize inevitability without inevitabilism.

Nothing surprises Yahuah.

Nothing interrupts His design.

Nothing advances without preparation.

QUOTE REFLECTION

Preparation is not reaction delayed — it is foresight revealed.

CORE REINFORCEMENT TERM III· MONTH 3
PRESERVATION, CORRUPTION, AND PROPHETIC FOREKNOWLEDGE

REINFORCEMENT PURPOSE

This Core Reinforcement consolidates the interpretive framework students must carry forward when reading Scripture through The Three Humanities lens. Month 3 trains the student how to discern preservation, corruption, and prophetic preparation in the biblical record, without collapsing timelines or importing later assumptions into earlier texts.

The goal is interpretive mastery, not content repetition.

GOVERNING INTERPRETIVE PRINCIPLES (MONTH 3)

Preservation Precedes Corruption

Scripture consistently establishes a pure standard before documenting deviation.

The First Humanity (Y+A=FH) is presented as:

- Ruach-bearing
- Covenant-capable
- Instructed
- Preserved intentionally

This preservation exists before the emergence of corruption, proving that corruption is not intrinsic to humanity but introduced.

Interpretive rule:

Never read corruption backward into preserved generations.

Corruption Is Identifiable Because Purity Was Documented

The emergence of The Second Humanity (AW + HW = N & NM + PW = N) is recognizable only because Scripture has already established:

- Lineage integrity
- Covenant continuity
- Ruach presence
- Instructional transmission

Without a preserved baseline, judgment would lack legitimacy.
Interpretive rule:
Judgment requires a documented standard of alignment.

Ruach, Not Behavior, Is the Primary Distinction
Month 3 clarifies a critical Yada Yahuah principle:
The defining boundary between humanities is not morality, intelligence, or power, but possession of the Ruach.
- The First Humanity (Y+A=FH) → Ruach-bearing, redeemable
- The Second Humanity (AW + HW = N & NM + PW = N) → flesh-only, non-redeemable

Interpretive rule:
Spiritual capacity determines covenant eligibility.

Genealogy Functions as Redemptive Architecture
Scriptural genealogies are structural, not sentimental.
They trace:
- Preservation of Ruach-bearing humanity
- Protection of redemptive continuity
- Containment of corruption

Month 3 reinforces that genealogy is how Scripture signals alignment, not ancestry.
Interpretive rule:
Scripture follows alignment, not population.

Prophetic Preparation Always Precedes Crisis
From Eden to the Flood, Yahuah reveals His pattern:
- Instruction before testing
- Memory before conflict
- Warning before judgment
- Preservation before cleansing

The rise of The Second Humanity (AW + HW = N & NM + PW = N) activates pre-existing protocols—it does not surprise heaven.

Interpretive rule:

Crisis reveals preparation already in place.

Integrated Interpretive Safeguards

Students must now actively avoid the following errors:

- Treating early humanity as naïve or undeveloped
- Assuming universal corruption before the Watchers' rebellion
- Moralizing what Scripture defines essentially
- Reading post-Flood realities into pre-Flood texts

Month 3 trains disciplined restraint in interpretation.

Continuity Statement

By the close of Term III – Month 3, the student should clearly understand:

- The First Humanity (Y+A=FH) was preserved intentionally, not temporarily
- The Second Humanity (AW + HW = N & NM + PW = N) represents an intrusion, not a continuation
- Redemption remains viable because preservation was secured in advance
- Judgment operates against a preserved standard, not a theoretical ideal

This framework prepares the student to engage Book Three without confusion, reactionism, or doctrinal drift.

TERM III · MONTH 4
MODULE OVERVIEW

The Three Humanities™ — Book 3: ***The Corruption of the Second Humanity (Irredeemable Humanity, Hybrid Lines, and the Equations of Existence)***

Term III · Month 4 advances the Three Humanities™ interpretive framework by examining The Second Humanity ***(AW + HW = N & NM + PW = N)*** in its fully corrupted and irredeemable state.

This module trains students to interpret Scripture according to created nature, inheritance, and covenant capacity, rather than moral behavior alone. It establishes why certain forms of corruption cannot be redeemed, why judgment escalates after the Flood, and why Scripture consistently follows the pure Adamic line while excluding hybrid lines from covenant continuity.

Month 4 does not collapse corruption into generic sin, nor does it universalize redemption. Instead, it clarifies how inheritance governs outcome, how mercy operates within judgment, and how post-Flood history must be read without projecting pre-Flood conditions backward or forward incorrectly.

This module also prepares the student for Term IV by completing the analytical framework of corruption, restraint, and irredeemability—without yet introducing the Third Humanity or its equation.

By the end of this month, the student will understand that:
- The Second Humanity (AW + HW = N & NM + PW = N) is defined by corrupted inheritance, not merely sinful behavior
- Corruption operates at the level of created nature and lineage
- Not all beings qualify for redemption within the same framework
- Mercy and judgment function together, not in opposition
- Hybrid corruption survives the Flood through restraint, not eradication

- Giants (Nephilim) reappear after the Flood through preserved corruption
- Scripture follows the pure Adamic line by design, not omission
- The Three Equations of Humanity govern destiny and outcome

This month answers why judgment intensifies and why restoration requires separation.

MODULE LEARNING OUTCOMES — TERM III · MONTH 4

By the end of Term III · Month 4, the student should be able to:

- Distinguish clearly between The First Humanity (Y+A=FH) and The Second Humanity (AW + HW = N & NM + PW = N) using Scriptural categories
- Demonstrate why The Second Humanity (AW + HW = N & NM + PW = N) is irredeemable based on inheritance and Ruach absence
- Explain how mercy and judgment operate together in the Flood and in post-Flood history
- Trace post-Flood corruption without collapsing it into pre-Flood hybridization
- Define and correctly apply the Three Equations of Humanity to destiny and outcome
- Articulate why Scripture tracks the pure Adamic line rather than hybrid lines

Mastery is demonstrated through disciplined interpretation, coherent synthesis, precise use of Scripture, and preservation of established doctrinal categories.

CHAPTER COVERAGE

Term III · Month 4 — The Three Humanities™ (Book 3)

- Week 45: Chapters 3–4

  Chapter 3 — Why The Second Humanity (AW + HW = N & NM + PW = N) Has No Redemption

  Chapter 4 — The Mercy of Yahuah Amid Rising Corruption

- Week 46: Chapters 5–6

  Chapter 5 — The Two-Part Redemptive Plan of Yahuah

  Chapter 6 — After the Flood: The Giants (Nephilim) Rise Again

- Week 47: Chapters 7–8
  Chapter 7 — Scripture Follows the Pure Line, Not the Hybrid One
  Chapter 8 — The Error of Qeynan (Kenan)
- Week 48: Chapters 9–10
  Chapter 9 — The Nephilim After the Flood
  Chapter 10 — The Three Equations of Humanity

THE PROPHETIC PURPOSE & HIDDEN PREPARATION FOR CONFLICT

Destiny Before Crisis

Purpose of Week 45

This week trains the student to identify prophetic preparation before visible crisis.

Scripture does not portray corruption as a sudden collapse but as a foreseen disruption anticipated long in advance. The existence of preserved lineage, prophetic knowledge, and covenant memory demonstrates that Yahuah prepares before He confronts.

Week 45 completes the study of The First Humanity (Yahuah → Adam = The First Humanity) and formally transitions the student into The Second Humanity (AW + HW = N & NM + PW = N) by establishing the governing interpretive principle:

Preservation always precedes judgment.

READ AND INSTRUCTION

Students must read the following texts before analysis.

- Bereshith (Genesis) 6:9

  Noach is identified as righteous and blameless within his generations. Students must determine why righteousness is qualified by lineage rather than behavior alone.

- Enoch 10:1–14

  Heaven responds to corruption with structured intervention, revealing that judgment is preceded by investigation, decree, and containment.

- Amos 3:7

  Yahuah reveals His purposes to His servants before action. Students must treat this as an interpretive rule, not a devotional statement.

Student Textbook Reading

The Three Humanities — Book 3

- Chapter 3: Why the Second Humanity Has No Redemption
- Chapter 4: The Mercy of Yahuah Amid Rising Corruption

These chapters establish the non-redeemable nature of The Second Humanity (AW + HW = N & NM + PW = N) and clarify why Noach becomes the vessel of continuity rather than a reformer of corruption.

Teaching Explanation

Students must learn to distinguish reactive judgment from prophetic preparation.

The emergence of The Second Humanity (AW + HW = N & NM + PW = N) is not treated in Scripture as an unexpected deviation. The preserved line of The First Humanity (Yahuah → Adam = The First Humanity), the advance warning given to Chanok, the sealing of judgment in heaven, and the pre-birth preparation of Noach all demonstrate foresight rather than reaction.

Interpretively, this establishes a critical rule of Yada Yahuah:

If judgment appears sudden in the text, preparation has already occurred off-stage.

Noach's designation as "perfect in his generations" must therefore be interpreted as lineage integrity, not moral flawlessness. Scripture measures preservation genealogically because redemption is transmitted through covenant continuity, not cultural reform.

Judgment, in this framework, is not corrective for corruption that can repent. It is protective removal of what cannot be redeemed.

Alignment Focus — Book 3, Chapters 3–4

Preparation Before Manifest Conflict

From Chapters 3 and 4, students must extract and articulate the following interpretive anchors:

- Non-Redeemability as a Category
  The Second Humanity (AW + HW = N & NM + PW = N) is defined by absence of Ruach, not moral failure.

- Why Mercy Targets Preservation, Not Reform
  Yahuah's mercy operates by securing the redeemable line, not attempting rehabilitation of what lacks covenant capacity.
- Lineage as the Battlefield of Redemption
  Conflict is genealogical before it is ethical.
- Noach as Evidence of Advance Preparation
  Noach's emergence demonstrates that preservation was in motion before judgment was announced.
- Heaven Acts Before Earth Reacts
  Revelation precedes catastrophe; judgment follows documentation.

KEY TERMS AND DEFINITIONS (WEEK 45)

- Prophetic Purpose
  Foreknowledge embedded into history to guide preservation and judgment.
- Preparation
  Intentional divine action established before crisis manifests.
- Conflict
  The inevitable confrontation between Ruach-bearing humanity and flesh-only corruption.

COVENANTAL STUDY TASK

Students must complete the following:

- **Explain why The Second Humanity (AW + HW = N & NM + PW = N)**
  is excluded from redemption using lineage and Ruach criteria
- **Demonstrate how prophetic preparation operates prior to visible crisis**
- **Interpret Bereshith 6:9 without importing post-biblical**
  assumptions about moral perfection

All answers must be derived directly from Scripture and assigned chapters.
Speculative frameworks are not permitted.

FINAL THOUGHTS ON WEEK 45

Judgment never interrupts the plan of Yahuah.

It executes what was already prepared.

QUOTE REFLECTION

"Preparation reveals sovereignty long before judgment reveals power."

INHERITANCE & IRREDEEMABILITY

Why the Second Humanity (AW + HW = N & NM + PW = N)
Has No Redemption

PURPOSE OF WEEK 46

This week trains the student to interpret inheritance as the governing category of redemption within the framework of Yada Yahuah.

Scripture does not present corruption as a behavioral problem correctable through instruction, reform, or moral appeal. Instead, it reveals corruption as a creational condition transmitted through lineage. This distinction explains why redemption is consistently extended to Adamic humanity but never to the hybrid race.

This week establishes the interpretive rule:

Yahuah redeems what He created and breathed into existence.

What originates outside His design is not repaired—it is removed.

Understanding this rule is essential for correctly reading the Flood, post-Flood history, and the continued confrontation with hybrid corruption.

Read and Instruction

- Bereshith (Genesis) 6:12
  "All flesh" refers to the totality of flesh within the corrupted hybrid lineage, demonstrating that corruption operated at the level of inheritance rather than individual moral failure.
- Enoch 15:8–12
  Hybrid beings are revealed as spirits born without the Ruach, incapable of repentance or restoration.
- Yochanan (John) 8:44
  Lineage is identified by nature, not by behavior or choice.
- Students must read these texts carefully and observe what Scripture attributes to nature rather than conduct.

Student Textbook Reading

The Three Humanities — Book 3

- Chapter 5 — The Two-Part Redemptive Plan of Yahuah
- Chapter 6 — After the Flood: The Giants (Nephilim) Rise Again

Students are not to summarize these chapters. They are to extract interpretive principles governing redemption, judgment, and preservation.

Teaching Explanation

Redemption in Scripture is restorative, not rehabilitative.

Yahuah restores what belongs to His original creation order. Adamic humanity—though capable of sin—retains the Ruach of Elohiym and therefore remains redeemable. By contrast, the Second Humanity (AW + HW = N & NM + PW = N) originates outside that order, having never received the Ruach, covenant capacity, nor spiritual inheritance required for repentance. Repentance is not withheld from them; it is structurally impossible for them.

Chapters 5 and 6 demonstrate that the Flood must be interpreted as redemptive surgery, not indiscriminate destruction. Preservation precedes judgment. The pure lineage is secured first; corruption is then removed. This sequence is consistent across Scripture.

The post-Flood reappearance of Giants (Nephilim) confirms that hybridization is not a closed historical episode but an ongoing creational threat requiring repeated restraint to protect the Messianic line.

The interpretive error this week corrects is the assumption that all beings described in Scripture are equally redeemable. Scripture never supports that claim.

Alignment Focus — Chapters 5 & 6

(Inheritance Determines Redemption)

From Chapters 5 and 6, students are to extract and articulate the following doctrinal anchors:

- Preservation Precedes Judgment

  Yahuah secures the covenant line before confronting corruption.

- Creational Origin Determines Redeemability
  The Second Humanity (AW + HW = N & NM + PW = N) lacks the Ruach and covenant structure required for redemption.
- The Flood as Redemptive Surgery
  What cannot be healed must be removed to preserve what can be redeemed.
- Inheritance Transmits Capacity
  Spiritual capacity is inherited, not learned or reformed into existence.
- Post-Flood Survival Confirms Ongoing Threat

The reappearance of Giants (Nephilim) demonstrates that corruption must be continually restrained to protect redemption.

KEY TERMS AND DEFINITIONS (WEEK 46)

- Inheritance
  The transmission of nature and spiritual capacity through lineage.
- Irredeemable
  Beyond restoration due to creational corruption.
- Hybridization
  Unlawful mixing that produces hybrid beings outside Yahuah's design.

COVENANTAL STUDY TASK

Pause your reading and complete the following:

•Explain why inheritance, not behavior, determines redeemability
•Identify why the Flood was necessary for salvation to continue
•Demonstrate how Scripture distinguishes between fallen humanity
and irredeemable corruption

Use Scripture and assigned chapters directly.

Avoid emotional, philosophical, or modern ethical assumptions.

FINAL THOUGHTS ON WEEK 46

Redemption restores what Yahuah created.

It does not redesign what rebellion produced.

The Second Humanity (AW + HW = N & NM + PW = N) was not rejected—it was never eligible.

QUOTE REFLECTION

"What was never pure cannot be restored."

MERCY, THE FLOOD, AND POST-FLOOD CORRUPTION
Judgment With Restraint

PURPOSE OF WEEK 47

This week trains the student to interpret Scripture's method, not merely its content, by identifying how mercy operates inside judgment and why corruption can reappear after a global cleansing.

The Flood did not erase memory, curiosity, or spiritual agency. Instead, it restrained domination, preserved covenant continuity, and limited corruption without abolishing human responsibility.

By engaging Chapters 7–8, students learn to read Scripture according to Yahuah's own narrative logic:

what is preserved, what is omitted, and why certain figures are highlighted while others disappear from the record.

READ AND INSTRUCTION

- Bereshith (Genesis) 6:8–9
  Favor and righteousness are identified within judgment, not outside it.
- Bereshith (Genesis) 9:20–27
  Post-Flood disorder emerges, demonstrating that cleansing does not eliminate agency.
- 2 Kepha (2 Peter) 2:4–5
  Judgment restrains rebellion but does not annihilate future accountability.

STUDENT TEXTBOOK READING

The Three Humanities — Book 3
- Chapter 7: Scripture Follows the Pure Line, Not the Hybrid One
- Chapter 8: The Error of Qeynan (Kenan): The Man Who Reopened the Door of Corruption

Students must read both chapters fully before analysis.

Teaching Explanation

Scripture Is Selective by Design

Chapter 7 establishes a governing interpretive principle:

Scripture is not a census of existence; it is a record of redemption.

This means:

- Omission does not equal nonexistence
- Inclusion signals covenant relevance
- Lineage is tracked by alignment, not population size or dominance

Students must therefore learn to read genealogies, silences, and narrative focus as intentional acts of revelation, not historical gaps.

Mercy Preserves Continuity, Not Innocence

The Flood functions as restraint, not erasure.

From Bereshith 6–9, judgment:

- Removes violent domination
- Preserves covenant capacity
- Resets order without deleting memory or desire

Mercy operates within judgment by safeguarding the line through which restoration remains possible, while allowing moral agency to persist.

Post-Flood Corruption Returns Through Knowledge, Not Immediate Force

Chapter 8 introduces a critical interpretive correction:

post-Flood corruption does not reassert itself first through physical domination or overt hybrid expansion, but through the preservation and transmission of forbidden knowledge.

Qeynan's error demonstrates that:

- What survives in memory can reactivate corruption
- Forbidden instruction can threaten covenant continuity as seriously as corrupted bloodlines
- Curiosity detached from obedience becomes an access point for rebellion
- Corruption often re-emerges covertly before it manifests overtly

This reframes post-Flood history not as the absence of corruption, but as a period in which corruption is restrained in expression while remaining accessible through knowledge.

Why Scripture Continues to Follow One Line

Because corruption resurfaces through teaching, Scripture responds by:

- Narrowing narrative focus
- Tracking obedience rather than influence
- Advancing covenant purpose instead of recording global activity

This is why figures like Qeynan appear briefly as warnings, while others *(Shem → Eber → Abram) are expanded as carriers of continuity.*

ALIGNMENT FOCUS – CHAPTERS 7 & 8

From these chapters, students must extract and apply:

- Selective Revelation as a Covenant Tool
- Mercy as Preservation, Not Permissiveness
- Judgment as Restraint, Not Obliteration
- Forbidden Knowledge as a Post-Judgment Threat
- Lineage Tracking as Redemptive Strategy

KEY TERMS AND DEFINITIONS (WEEK 47)

- Mercy
  Yahuah's intentional safeguarding of His created order and covenant purpose before, during, and beyond judgment.
- Restraint
  Limitation of corruption without elimination of agency.
- Selective Revelation
  Yahuah's intentional focus on what advances redemption.
- Resurgence
  Return of corruption through memory and knowledge rather than force.

COVENANTAL STUDY TASK

Pause and complete the following:

- **Explain why Scripture omits vast populations while preserving narrow genealogies**
- **Demonstrate how mercy functions inside judgment rather than opposing it**
- **Identify how post-Flood corruption re-enters through knowledge transmission**
- **Show why Scripture continues to follow covenant alignment instead of power structures**

Use Scripture and assigned chapters directly.
Avoid speculative history or philosophical abstraction.

FINAL THOUGHTS ON WEEK 47

Judgment limits destruction.

Mercy secures the future.

Scripture follows alignment, not aftermath.

QUOTE REFLECTION

"Judgment restrains evil; it does not erase choice."

TERM III· MONTH 4 — WEEK 48
PURE LINE, GIANTS (NEPHILIM), AND THE THREE EQUATIONS
Destiny Determined by Nature

PURPOSE OF WEEK 48

This final week trains students to interpret why Scripture tracks covenant continuity through selected lineage and why hybrid lines are acknowledged but never centered. Interpretation is governed by the equation framework, not by assumptions about fairness, population size, or narrative completeness.

Students will apply the governing model:
- The First Humanity $(Y+A=FH)$
- The Second Humanity $(AW + HW = N$ & $NM + PW = N)$

Read and Instruction
- Bereshith (Genesis) 10:8–9
  Read to identify how post-Flood rebellion becomes centralized and institutional. Students must interpret Nimrod as a signal of trajectory, not merely a character.
- Bemidbar (Numbers) 13:33
  Read to confirm that hybrid continuation remains a Scripture-recognized reality after the Flood. Interpretation must stay anchored to inheritance, not spectacle.
- Mattityahu (Matthew) 13:24–30
  Read to interpret coexistence without confusion: covenant line and corrupt line can occupy the same world while remaining distinct until separation.

Required Textbook Reading — The Three Humanities, Book Three
- Chapter 9 — The Nephilim After the Flood
- Chapter 10 — The Three Equations of Humanity
Students must read both chapters before analysis.

Teaching Explanation

Scripture is Covenant-Selective

Scripture does not attempt to preserve a full record of all populations. It preserves the line that carries covenant continuity and the capacity for Yada Yahuah.

Therefore, students must interpret selective genealogies as alignment-tracking, not omission.

This interpretive rule is governed by:

- The First Humanity *(Y+A=FH)*

Giants (Nephilim) Are "Collision Evidence," Not Covenant Subjects

When Giants (Nephilim) appear in the text, the purpose is not to shift focus to them, but to document collision against the covenant stream.

Giants (Nephilim) are referenced as a threat-pattern that emerges from:

- The Second Humanity *(AW + HW = N & NM + PW = N)*

Students must not treat "Giants (Nephilim)" as an alternate covenant storyline. They are included only when they intersect with covenant continuity.

Inheritance Governs Outcome

Interpretation must treat corruption as an inheritance-condition, not as a behavioral category.

This week requires students to use the equation model as the interpretive filter:

THE FIRST HUMANITY

Humanity Equation *(Y+A=FH)*

Yahuah → Adam = The First Humanity

(Spirit-first, pure, incorruptible origin)

THE SECOND HUMANITY

Humanity Equations *(AW + HW = N & NM + PW = N)*

1.   Angels Watchers + Human Women = Nephilim
2.   Nephilim Men + Pure Women = More Nephilim

Students must treat these equations as governing categories for:

- covenant eligibility
- redemptive capacity
- narrative emphasis
- judgment boundaries

ALIGNMENT FOCUS – CHAPTERS 9 & 10

(Lineage, Corruption, and Outcome)

- From Chapters 9 and 10, students must extract the following anchors and express them as interpretive controls:
- Scripture tracks covenant continuity through The First Humanity (Y+A=FH), not through numerical dominance.
- Post-Flood hybrid survival is interpreted through The Second Humanity (AW + HW = N & NM + PW = N), not through mythic exaggeration.
- Babel functions as organized resurgence: interpret Babel as structural rebellion rather than "city-building."
- Giants (Nephilim) reappear as proof of continuation, requiring disciplined lineage analysis rather than moral generalization.
- The Three Equations operate as interpretive law, not optional symbolism.

KEY TERMS AND DEFINITIONS (WEEK 48)

- Covenant-Selective Record
  Scripture records what preserves covenant continuity through The First Humanity (Y+A=FH).
  Hybrid Continuation
- Post-Flood persistence explained through The Second Humanity (AW + HW = N & NM + PW = N).
- Equation-Based Interpretation
  A disciplined interpretive method where lineage, capacity, and narrative emphasis are interpreted through the governing equations rather than through assumptions.

COVENANTAL STUDY TASK

Pause your reading and complete the following:

1.**Using Bereshith 10:8–9, identify what Nimrod represents in post-Flood trajectory and explain why Scripture records him at all (interpretive relevance).**

2.**Using Bemidbar 13:33, demonstrate why the appearance of Giants (Nephilim) must be interpreted through:**
• **The Second Humanity (AW + HW = N & NM + PW = N)**

3.**Using Mattityahu 13:24–30, explain how coexistence can occur without covenant merging. Your answer must show how covenant continuity remains traceable through:**
• **The First Humanity (Y+A=FH)**

Restriction: Do not argue from emotion, fairness categories, or modern population assumptions. Interpretation must remain inside the equation framework.

FINAL THOUGHTS ON WEEK 48

This week closes Term III by requiring students to interpret Scripture through covenant continuity and inheritance law rather than through surface-level events.

Interpretation remains governed by:

THE FIRST HUMANITY (Y+A=FH)

The Second Humanity (AW + HW = N & NM + PW = N)

CORE REINFORCEMENT
TERM III · MONTH 4
Inheritance, Irredeemability, and Covenant Restraint

REINFORCEMENT PURPOSE

This Core Reinforcement consolidates the interpretive framework students must carry forward when engaging post-Flood Scripture through The Three Humanities lens.

Month 4 trains the student to distinguish inheritance-based destiny from behavior-based evaluation, and to read judgment, mercy, and restraint without collapsing categories or introducing unauthorized assumptions.

The goal remains interpretive mastery, not content repetition.

Governing Interpretive Principles (Month 4)

INHERITANCE DETERMINES REDEEMABILITY

Scripture presents redemption as restoration to an original created state, not rehabilitation of every existing being.

- The First Humanity (Y+A=FH)
    - → Ruach-bearing
    - → Covenant-capable
    - → Redeemable despite fall
- The Second Humanity (AW + HW = N & NM + PW = N)
    - → Flesh-only
    - → No Ruach
    - → Outside covenant
    - → Non-redeemable

Month 4 establishes that what is not authored by Yahuah cannot be restored by redemption.

Never treat redeemability as a moral category; it is a creational one.

Judgment Functions as Preservation, Not Erasure Scripture reveals that judgment consistently operates with restraint.

- The Flood removed irredeemable corruption
- The Flood preserved covenant continuity
- Babel restrained unified rebellion without annihilating humanity

Judgment limits corruption without eliminating agency, memory, or future testing.

Judgment restrains what threatens redemption; it does not reset history to innocence.

Scripture Tracks Covenant Capacity, Not Historical Exhaustiveness
Month 4 reinforces that the biblical record is covenantal, not encyclopedic.

Scripture follows:

- Ruach-bearing lineage
- Covenant carriers
- Redemptive continuity

It does not follow:

- Hybrid dominion
- Corrupted populations
- Irredeemable bloodlines

The absence of detail is intentional, not accidental.

What Scripture does not track is not denied — it is disqualified.

Mercy Operates Inside Judgment
Mercy is not the suspension of justice; it is the preservation of possibility.

- Noach is preserved while the world collapses
- Languages are confused to prevent total corruption
- Hybrid domination is restrained repeatedly

Mercy ensures that redemption remains viable even when corruption resurfaces.

Mercy safeguards the future while judgment addresses the present.

Corruption Can Re-emerge Without Repeating the Original Cause

Month 4 corrects a common interpretive error:

The return of corruption after the Flood does not require a second Watchers descent.

It emerges through:

- Surviving hybrid line
- Forbidden knowledge
- Human transmission
- Covenant abandonment

This distinction prevents misreading post-Flood history as a replay instead of a progression.

Resurgence does not equal repetition.

Integrated Interpretive Safeguards

Students must now actively avoid the following errors:

- Treating redemption as universally available
- Assuming judgment eliminates future rebellion
- Moralizing beings Scripture defines essentially
- Tracking power, size, or influence instead of covenant capacity
- Introducing unauthorized equations or premature humanities

Month 4 reinforces interpretive restraint under complexity.

Continuity Statement

By the close of Term III · Month 4, the student should clearly understand:

- The First Humanity *(Y+A=FH)* remains the only fully redeemable human category
- The Second Humanity *(AW + HW = N & NM + PW = N)* remains permanently outside redemption
- Judgment functions to protect salvation, not to express reaction
- Scripture follows the line that can be restored, not every line that exists
- This framework prepares the student to advance without narrative drift, Yada

Yahuah improvisation, or equation misuse as the course progresses.

TERM III · MONTH 4 — MASTER-LEVEL ESSAY

Pinnacle Assessment · Irredeemability, Inheritance, and the Equations of Humanity

Length: 1,800–2,200 words

Status: REQUIRED

Essay Prompt — Month 4

Using the Three Equations of Humanity, explain why Scripture presents redemption as inheritance-dependent rather than universally applicable, and demonstrate how judgment, mercy, and restraint function together to preserve covenant continuity.

Your essay must:

- Clearly define and apply:
  - The First Humanity (Y+A=FH)
  - The Second Humanity (AW + HW = N & NM + PW = N)
- Demonstrate why Ruach-bearing capacity, not moral behavior, determines redeemability
- Explain why The Second Humanity is irredeemable by nature, not by refusal or severity of sin
- Analyze the Flood as redemptive surgery, not indiscriminate punishment
- Trace how post-Flood corruption re-emerges through inheritance and knowledge rather than a second Watcher descent
- Defend why Scripture:
  - follows the pure Adamic line
  - acknowledges but never centers hybrid lines
- Apply the equation framework as interpretive law, not symbolic language

Constraints

- Use Scripture and The Three Humanities (Book 3) only
- Do not argue from:
  - emotional fairness
  - universalist assumptions
  - ophilosophical anthropology

- Maintain equation-based interpretation at all times

Evaluation Criteria
- Precision in defining humanity categories
- Correct application of inheritance logic
- Clear distinction between mercy, judgment, and restraint
- Faithful handling of post-Flood continuity
- Demonstrated Master-level command of irreedeemability without moralization

CONCLUSION — BOOK 3 ↠ BOOK 4

Transition to MBRS Book 4 — Master-Level Foundations

MBRS Book 3 has established the indispensable interpretive architecture of The Three Humanities™. Creation has been secured as complete, ordered, and sanctified. The First Humanity has been traced as preserved, Ruach-bearing, and covenant-capable. The emergence of corruption has been identified not as moral failure alone, but as intrusion into created order. Lineage has been revealed as covenant architecture. Preservation has been shown to precede judgment. Preparation has been demonstrated before crisis.

At this stage, the student possesses the structural controls necessary to read Scripture without collapsing categories, importing assumptions, or misplacing corruption in the wrong epoch. The equations governing humanity have been introduced. The distinction between redeemable and irredeemable inheritance has been established. The narrative field is now fully prepared.
Yet foundational mastery is not the final task.

The next stage advances into Master-Level Advanced analysis, where the full implications of irredeemable corruption, hybrid inheritance, judgment, mercy, restraint, and covenant continuity are examined in their mature form. MBRS Book 4 therefore carries the student beyond foundational structure into advanced application — where the equations of humanity, the operations of judgment, and the safeguarding of redemption are explored in complete depth.

The student now moves from foundational mastery into advanced covenantal discernment.

TERM III — GLOSSARY

Apokryfos: A designation meaning "hidden away," used for ancient writings that were preserved yet later excluded or marginalized by religious systems. In this Institute, Apokryfos writings are evaluated by content, consistency with Dabar, and covenantal themes, not by later tradition and these writings do not replace the Tôrâh but testify to its fulfillment. Writings preserved under covenantal guardianship that were intentionally safeguarded rather than broadly circulated. The term "hidden" refers to the method and timing of preservation, not to a lack of spiritual value or authority within covenant instruction.

Author of the Heavenly Tablets: Yahuah Himself. The authority and permanence of the Heavenly Tablets rest solely on His authorship, not on human transmission.

Book of Enoch: A collection of ancient writings attributed to Chanok (Enoch), addressing heavenly revelation, judgment, rebellion, and divine instruction. In this module, Enoch is used to examine pre-Sinai instruction, heavenly record, and the conflict between truth and corruption.

Book of Jubilees: An ancient Hebrew work closely aligned with Genesis and Exodus, emphasizing covenant order, commandments, appointed times, and heavenly record. In this module, Jubilees is used to support the concepts of heavenly testimony, continuity of Tôrâh, and preservation beyond human institutions.

Canon (Reframed as Tôrâh): The term canon is a Greek construct historically used by human systems to define, limit, alter, or exclude inspired writings through institutional authority. In Yada Yahuah, canon is not determined by councils, traditions, or classification, but by divine authorship and covenantal preservation. Therefore, the true and only canon is Tôrâh—the authoritative instruction originating with Yahuah Himself. Tôrâh defines the boundary of inspired instruction because its source is divine, not because it has been ratified or measured by humanity. Any use of the term canon must be understood as subordinate to, and corrected by, Tôrâh as the original and governing standard of Scripture.

Concealment: The deliberate withholding of revelation by Yahuah until an appointed covenantal time, ensuring that preserved instruction is revealed according to divine purpose rather than human readiness or demand.

Continuity of Meaning: The faithful preservation of covenant doctrine through language, in which key terms retain their intended meaning across generations, writings, and administrations without contradiction.

Corrupt Priesthood: A priestly authority that has been compromised and ultimately removed due to disobedience, self-interest, boundary violation, or usurpation of covenant office. A corrupt priesthood may retain outward title, lineage, ritual function, or institutional recognition while lacking covenantal authorization from Yahuah. This includes historical usurpers such as the Hasmonean priesthood, figures identified in Scripture as the Wicked Priest, and any subsequent religious system—ancient or modern—that assumes priestly authority apart from divine appointment. Such systems often operate within broader Babel structures, preserving form while severing allegiance to Yahuah's Tôrâh, thereby misleading the people through illegitimate governance of worship and instruction.

Covenant-Selective Record: Scripture records history not to explain humanity, but to preserve Yahuah's covenant purpose through the unaltered line of The First Humanity Y+A=FH), documenting only what serves, threatens, or restores that purpose.

Cumulative Corruption: rebellion originating in Watcher angel transgression, preserved and transmitted through illicit teaching, forbidden knowledge, and corrupted lineage, and progressively matured across generations of humanity. It describes the long arc by which Watcher instruction, once introduced in Genesis through boundary violation and unlawful union, continues to shape systems, worship, governance, and belief until corruption becomes global, public, and entrenched. Cumulative corruption is not episodic or accidental; it is instructional, inherited, and institutionalized. Across the ages, corrupted knowledge is repackaged, normalized, and embedded into religious, political, and cultural systems—forming enduring Babel structures that sustain rebellion even after judgment events. By the end of the age, corruption is no longer isolated behavior but a self-sustaining order, preserved through systems rather than bodies, and requiring final divine judgment.

Darkness: Departure from divine alignment while remaining human, sustained and intensified through the influence of evil spirits originating from pre-Flood hybrid corruption. Darkness is not the loss of humanity, but the condition in which human perception, desire, and worship are shaped by deceptive spiritual influence rather than by Yahuah's instruction. Darkness operates through distortion, concealment, and substitution—preserving outward humanity while redirecting allegiance, understanding, and practice away from Yahuah's Tôrâh. It represents the ongoing, non-embodied continuation of Watcher rebellion within human systems, belief structures, and consciousness.

Deception: The mechanism through which disobedience is introduced by the deliberate mixture of truth with falsehood. Deception does not operate through outright denial of truth, but through partial truth, reframing, and selective omission, creating confusion that obscures consequence and redefines obedience. By blending what is true with what is false, deception destabilizes discernment, redirects trust, and gradually leads the subject toward transgression while maintaining the appearance of legitimacy. The final act of disobedience is therefore not sudden, but the culmination of progressive distortion.

Decretive Judgment: judgment established against an enduring corrupt outcome

Deluge: A judicial act of cleansing and containment, not corrective discipline.

Demonic Spirits: Disembodied spirits originating from the offspring of illicit unions between Watcher angels and human women. When the hybrid beings (Nephilim) were destroyed in the Flood, their embodied form perished, but their spirits remained bound to the earth. These spirits now operate without flesh, exerting influence rather than embodiment, and function as continuing agents of deception, corruption, and rebellion. Demonic spirits perpetuate the Watcher legacy by influencing belief, worship, and behavior, seeking expression through systems, possession, intimidation, and distortion of truth. They do not possess covenant inheritance, rest, or authority, but persist as residual corruption until final judgment.

Disembodied Corruption: Rebellion operating without embodied form through evil spirits, demonic influence, and the systems they animate rather than through fleshly beings. Disembodied corruption originates from the spirits of hybrid offspring produced by illicit Watcher–human unions, whose bodies were destroyed but whose influence persisted after judgment. These spirits propagate rebellion by inhabiting, empowering, and sustaining religious, political, economic, and ideological systems, allowing corruption to continue across generations without dependence on altered biology. Disembodied corruption functions through deception, institutional memory, doctrine, and authority structures, making rebellion durable, transferable, and resistant to reform until final judgment.

Disobedience: Violation of divine instruction without alteration of created nature

Evil Spirits (Demons): Bodiless spirits of the Nephilim, confined to the earth without inheritance or rest.

Farmakía (φαρμακεία): Engineered deception originating in ancient sorcery and potions, now continued through chemical substances, drugs, and pharmaceutical systems that alter perception, dependence, and conscience. Farmakía refers to the use of substances and systems to manipulate belief, behavior, worship, and submission by chemically and psychologically conditioning populations. In its ancient form, farmakía involved witchcraft, potions, and enchantments used to control, seduce, or deceive. In its modern expression, farmakía is institutionalized through medical, pharmaceutical, and regulatory systems that function as a new form of witchcraft—replacing ritual potions with chemical compounds, and personal sorcerers with authorized institutions. Though presented as healing or progress, farmakía operates as spiritual control when it substitutes trust in Yahuah, alters discernment, or enforces dependence through deception and coercion. Farmakía is therefore not limited to occult ritual; it is the systemic practice of spiritual manipulation through substances and structures that dull discernment, normalize submission, and advance rebellion under the appearance of legitimacy.

Flood: A global act of divine judgment designed to cleanse creation from irreversible corruption by wiping out the pervasive Nephilim hybrid presence while preserving the covenant bloodline. The Flood was enacted to protect the seed of the covenant—the uncorrupted human lineage through which Yahuah's purpose and restoration would continue—rather than to annihilate humanity indiscriminately. This cleansing targeted corrupted flesh, altered lineage, and hybrid domination that had filled the world, ensuring that creation could be reset to a state where covenant continuity remained possible. The Flood therefore functioned as containment and preservation, not merely punishment, removing embodied corruption while safeguarding the future of restoration.

Fullness (of corruption): The terminal stage of corruption in which hybridized humanity, altered nature, and rebellion have reached complete concentration, normalization, and self-sustainment, leaving no remaining capacity for repentance, restoration, or covenant continuity. Fullness marks the point at which corruption has accomplished all it can accomplish and nothing further can be added, corrected, or reversed. In this state—seen historically in hybrid-dominated humanity—corruption is no longer episodic or contested; it is total, inherited, institutionalized, and biologically entrenched. Because there is no path back, Yahuah's intervention through judgment becomes necessary, not punitive, to preserve what remains of creation and to prevent irreversible spread. Fullness therefore triggers judgment not because evil is increasing, but because evil has completed its course.

Genealogical Confrontation: The moment at which pure Adamic seed encounters corrupted Nephilim seed, forcing the issue of origin rather than behavior. Genealogical confrontation occurs when lineage, not conduct, becomes the determining factor of covenant viability—resulting in the emergence of a third, mixed humanity produced by the union of uncorrupted human lineage with corrupted Nephilim inheritance. This confrontation exposes that corruption is not resolved through moral correction or obedience alone, because the conflict lies in nature and origin, not actions. Genealogical confrontation therefore marks a decisive shift in covenant history, where preservation, judgment, or separation must occur to address incompatibility at the level of seed.

Genealogy: A structural record that traces lineage, origin, and transmission of nature across generations. Genealogy demonstrates continuity of covenant purpose when the seed remains uncorrupted, but it also exposes the transfer of hybrid or mixed genes when corrupted lineage is introduced. In Scripture, genealogy functions as a diagnostic tool, revealing whether life, authority, and inheritance proceed from pure Adamic origin, corrupted Nephilim lineage, or mixed humanity. Genealogy therefore records not only purpose and identity, but the biological and spiritual condition that determines covenant capacity, compatibility, and continuity.

Giants (Nephilim): Embodied descendants of Nephilim bloodlines originating from illicit unions between Watcher angels and human women. Giants represent the most visible and extreme expression of Nephilim hybridization due to their size, strength, and domination, but they are not the only form of corrupted offspring. The term giants is often emphasized because of their prominence and threat, yet Nephilim corruption produced multiple kinds of hybrid descendants, not all of whom manifested extraordinary stature. Many corrupted offspring appeared outwardly human while still carrying altered nature, hybrid inheritance, and covenant incompatibility. Scripture highlights giants because they are unmistakable, but the broader issue is corrupted seed, not size. Giants therefore function as evidence, not definition, of Nephilim presence. They expose the reality of hybrid corruption that extended far beyond what was immediately visible.

Half-Truth: A deliberate mixture in which truth is combined with even a small measure of falsehood, rendering it no longer truth at all, but deception. A half-truth retains enough accuracy to appear credible while introducing distortion that obscures consequence, alters meaning, and redirects trust. Because truth is 100% pure, anything less than complete truth functions as a lie. The Nachash employed half-truth by affirming elements of Yahuah's word while reframing intent and consequence, inserting doubt without outright denial. Half-truth is therefore deception's most effective tool, as it conceals rebellion beneath familiarity and plausibility.

Hybrid Continuation: The post-Flood persistence of Nephilim corruption through The Second Humanity, resulting from successive illicit unions: first between Watcher Angels and Human Women (AW + HW = N) producing Nephilim, and subsequently between Nephilim Men and Pure Women (NM + PW = N). Although the Flood eliminated the dominant embodied Nephilim presence, hybrid corruption was not entirely erased, as altered seed survived through concealed lineage transmission. Hybrid continuation explains how corrupted genetics, nature, and influence reemerged after the Flood, not through renewed Watcher descent alone, but through surviving hybrid bloodlines integrated into post-Flood humanity. This continuation accounts for the reappearance of giants, corrupted peoples, and covenant conflict in later generations, demonstrating that judgment removed dominance but did not immediately eliminate all corrupted seed.

Hybrid Corruption (Nephilim): The contamination of the created order through unlawful union between Watcher angels and human women, producing Nephilim—hybrid beings whose existence altered flesh, lineage, and covenant capacity. Hybrid corruption is not metaphorical or moral alone; it is a creational violation in which incompatible realms were merged, resulting in beings and bloodlines outside Yahuah's design. This corruption introduced altered nature into humanity, disrupted genealogical purity, and generated offspring whose inheritance could not participate in covenant restoration. Hybrid corruption therefore represents a direct assault on creation itself, necessitating containment, judgment, and preservation of uncorrupted seed.

Hybridization: An unlawful mixture that violates Yahuah's divine assignment by combining what was created to remain distinct. Hybridization occurs biologically through the mixing of Nephilim bloodline with pure Adamic seed, producing hybrid or mixed humanity, and it also occurs instructionally through the transmission of forbidden knowledge, Watcher teachings, and heavenly mysteries fused with human culture.

Whether enacted through flesh or through teaching, hybridization produces corrupt fruit, alters nature, distorts purpose, and compromises covenant capacity. Biological hybridization corrupts lineage and inheritance; instructional hybridization corrupts worship, perception, and alignment—yet both proceed from the same rebellion against divine boundaries. Hybridization therefore explains the continuation of Nephilim corruption after judgment events, as corrupted seed and corrupted instruction work together to preserve rebellion across generations.

Idolatry: The giving of worship, allegiance, or covenant participation to any power, system, being, or practice other than Yahuah, including the mixing of truth with falsehood and the mixing of pure Adamic seed with corrupted Nephilim lineage. Idolatry operates through the worship of demons and evil spirits disguised as gods, as well as through ideologies, institutions, traditions, or unions that violate Yahuah's boundaries. This includes the prohibited practice of pure men uniting with Nephilim women, which constitutes idolatry because it merges covenant seed with corrupted origin, transferring allegiance, inheritance, and continuity away from Yahuah's design. Such unions are not merely biological violations but covenantal betrayals, just as false worship is a spiritual betrayal.

Idolatry therefore functions both spiritually and genealogically:

• Spiritually, by redirecting worship and belief through deception and mixture

• Genealogically, by corrupting lineage through unlawful union

All forms of idolatry ultimately serve demonic influence and Watcher legacy, whether expressed through worship, belief systems, institutions, or seed mixture, because they replace exclusive covenant loyalty to Yahuah with substituted authority and corrupted continuity.

Indwelling: Permanent Spirit presence establishing identity and life.

Institutional Continuity: Persistence of influence through law, ritual, and authority.

Interpretive Collapse: The error of assigning later-defined conditions to earlier textual states.

Irredeemable: Beyond restoration due to creational corruption.

Judgment: Divine containment of irreversible corruption through authoritative decree and restraint. Boundary enforcement that ends corruption's access and secures restored order. Boundary enforcement required when corruption becomes total and publicly enthroned. In Week 30, judgment is not divine volatility; it is the necessary covenant act that ends an irreversible system when rebellion reaches full maturation.

Lineage: The transmission of nature, inheritance, and capacity through flesh and genealogy. Lineage may preserve pure Adamic seed aligned with Yahuah's covenant purpose, or it may transmit corrupted inheritance resulting from Nephilim hybridization and rebellion. Scripture treats lineage as a covenantal determinant because origin matters: pure lineage sustains covenant continuity, while corrupted lineage compromises or disqualifies covenant capacity. Lineage therefore functions as both preservation and exposure—revealing whether continuity flows from divine design or from altered, hybrid origin.

Malkîy-Tsedeq Priesthood: Eternal priesthood fulfilled in Yahusha

Maśṭêmâh: An authorized angelic agent overseeing permitted testing and accusation under divine limit. An authorized angelic agent tasked with testing, accusation, and execution under limit

Mixture: The unlawful blending of what Yahuah has ordered to remain distinct, resulting in distortion of purpose and nature.

Nachash: A deceiving agent belonging to a category of light-bearing angelic beings, not a serpent creature. Nachash operates through reframing truth by distortion, not through outright denial. By presenting truth with altered emphasis, omitted consequence, or redirected intent, Nachash introduces doubt while maintaining the appearance of legitimacy. Nachash's deception functions through speech, instruction, and persuasion, targeting perception rather than force. The association with a "serpent" is descriptive of function (crafty, subtle, penetrating), not biological form. As a light-being, Nachash was capable of communication, reasoning, and Yada Yahuah reframing, making deception effective precisely because it appeared enlightened rather than hostile.

Nephilim: Hybrid beings originating from unlawful Watcher–human unions

New Creation: Transformation of nature rather than correction of behavior. An introduced humanity with a distinct origin, not an improved form of the old.

New Yarushalayim: The promised dwelling place of Yahuah with the righteous, depicted as descending to earth, where covenant restoration, righteousness, and divine presence are fully realized rather than escaped from creation.

Occult Systems: Frameworks originating in Watcher transmission, marked by secrecy and control

Pornía (πορνεία): The comprehensive expression of covenant betrayal, encompassing all forms of evil that present themselves as legitimate, righteous, or divinely sanctioned. Pornía is not limited to sexual immorality; it includes false worship, idolatry, unlawful unions, doctrinal mixture, institutional corruption, and alliance with illegitimate authority—all masquerading as faithfulness. In the New Testament, and especially in Apokálypsis, pornía functions as a totalizing category of rebellion, describing how deception engulfs belief, worship, governance, and identity. It is spiritual prostitution:

the abandonment of exclusive covenant loyalty to Yahuah in exchange for power, protection, legitimacy, or survival within corrupted systems. Pornía therefore gathers every manifestation of evil—biological, spiritual, instructional, and institutional—into a single covenantal verdict: violation presented as righteousness. Through pornía, nations are seduced into mistaking corruption for obedience and rebellion for faithfulness.

Post-Flood Corruption: Reemergence of disorder through bloodline, spirits, deception, and systems

Pre-Manifest Existence: Existence assigned by Yahuah prior to physical appearance in time.

Priestly Guardianship: Covenant-appointed stewardship of Dabar Yahuah

Priesthood: The covenant-appointed order set apart to minister before Yahuah and to teach, preserve, and administer His Tôrâh among the people. Priesthood is not merely religious leadership; it is an authorized covenant office with defined responsibilities and boundaries.

Removal: Termination of corruption that cannot inherit covenant purpose.

Remnant Corruption: Residual Nephilim bloodline and Watcher-derived teachings that survive judgment, allowing corrupted lineage, knowledge, and influence to persist, reemerge, and propagate rebellion across subsequent generations.

Replacement: Installation of aligned carriers capable of sustaining covenant execution.

Resurgence: Return of corruption through memory and knowledge rather than force.

Restoration: Replacement of corrupted alignment through divine calling. The irreversible release of creation into its original design once corruption is removed.

Rebellion: is the organized departure from Yahuah's order, originating in Watcher transgression and perpetuated through unauthorized teaching, boundary violation, and distorted knowledge. Rebellion alienates humanity from Yahuah's true Tôrâh by introducing alternative structures, narratives, and systems that mimic authority while severing covenant alignment. Rebellion may use systems, teachings, and even administrative forms, but it is defined by origin and allegiance, not by structure.

Seed War: The ongoing creational conflict between the pure Adamic bloodline and instruction aligned with Yahuah, and the corrupted Nephilim and adversarial bloodlines and teachings that oppose covenant continuity. The Seed War is fought through lineage, worship, belief, instruction, and authority, not merely through violence, and culminates in final judgment when corrupted seed and doctrine are permanently removed.

Spiritual Intoxication: The condition in which discernment is impaired through sustained exposure to Babel's redefined devotion. Spiritual intoxication explains why nations are "drunk": not lacking truth entirely, but rendered unable to distinguish covenant obedience from sanctioned corruption.

Spiritual Warfare: Resistance to deception through truth, obedience, and alignment with the Word.

Systemic Rebellion: Organized deception embedded within religious, political, economic, and instructional authority structures, through which rebellion against Yahuah is normalized, preserved, and enforced. Systemic rebellion operates by redefining legitimacy, blending truth with falsehood, and institutionalizing corrupted teaching so that opposition to Yahuah's order appears lawful, righteous, and necessary.

Third Humanity: Produced by the post-Flood union of Pure Men and Nephilim Women (PM + NW= MH), in which the Pure Man transmits the Ruach and the Nephilim Woman transmits corrupted inheritance, resulting in a partially corrupted, internally divided human condition with the capacity to incline either toward Yahuah or toward evil.

Throne (of Babel): The matured form of post-Flood rebellion in which defiance is no longer localized by proximity (tower), but institutionalized through governance, worship, economy, and doctrine. The throne represents centralized authority that rules by regulation and redefinition rather than chaotic violence.

Tôrâh (תּוֹרָה): Instruction, law, or teaching issued by Yahuah. Tôrâh represents the true rule and measure of divine authority, existing prior to and beyond later human categorizations.

Transmission: The passing of influence, knowledge, or corruption from one party to another through instruction, imitation, or participation.

Two Kinds of Humanity: Two spiritual conditions of human existence, not two creations

Universal Defiance: The final stage of rebellion in which kings, nations, merchants, and religious structures are unified under Babel's redefinition of worship and authority. Universal defiance is not merely widespread sin, but coordinated covenant opposition through shared system.

Violence: The outward manifestation of corruption consuming humanity and creation.

Watcher Angels: Authorized emissaries originally appointed by Yahuah to observe, instruct, and testify to humanity regarding judgment, order, and uprightness. These same beings later violated their assigned nature and authority, corrupting themselves through unlawful union with human women and the transmission of forbidden knowledge, thereby initiating hybrid corruption and rebellion. As a result of this transgression, the Watcher angels were confined and restrained, removed from their former function and locked away awaiting final judgment, unable to continue direct interaction with humanity. Their rebellion nevertheless persists indirectly through the legacy of corrupted lineage, teachings, and disembodied spirits that followed their fall.

Watcher Legacy: The ongoing transmission of corruption through hidden teachings, forbidden knowledge, and revealed mysteries given by the Watcher angels to humanity—teachings never intended for human possession or use. This legacy persists through instruction rather than embodiment, leading humanity into deception, mixture, and ultimately perdition, because such knowledge exceeds human assignment and violates divine order.

Humanity Framework (Alphabetized by Entry Name)

The First Humanity: (Y + A = FH):

Yahuah → Adam = First Humanity

Spirit-first, pure, incorruptible origin. The First Humanity is created directly by the Ruach of Yahuah.

The Second Humanity: (AW + HW = N & NM + PW = N)

Humanity altered through corruption introduced by Watcher rebellion

Angel Watchers + Human Women = Nephilim and Nephilim Men + Pure Women = Continued Hybridization. The Second Humanity is not fallen humanity — it is altered humanity.

The Third Humanity: (PM + NW = MH)

Pure Men + Nephilim Women = Mixed Humanity. This is not restoration. This is biological humanity restored, but spiritually damaged.

The Third Humanity — The Variant: (Y $\oplus$ HW = Y)

Yahuah (Ruach) + Human Woman (Miryam) = Yahusha. The New Spiritual Humanity is born

The Return to the First Humanity: (Y + RT = FH):

Yahusha (the perfected Variant) + Resurrection Transf

www.ingramcontent.com/pod-product-compliance
Lightning Source LLC
Chambersburg PA
CBHW080608090426
42735CB00017B/3366